MW01105188

A Legacy of Faith

Annette B. Sutcliffe

with Cindy McKeowen

WESTBOW
PRESS®
A DIVISION OF THOMAS NELSON
& ZONDERVAN

This book is a work of non-fiction. Unless otherwise noted, the author and the publisher make no explicit guarantees as to the accuracy of the information contained in this book and in some cases, names of people and places have been altered to protect their privacy.

Scripture quotations taken from the New American Standard Bible® (NASB), Copyright © 1960, 1962, 1963, 1968, 1971, 1972, 1973, 1975, 1977, 1995 by The Lockman Foundation Used by permission. www.Lockman.org

WestBow Press books may be ordered through booksellers or by contacting:

WestBow Press
A Division of Thomas Nelson & Zondervan
1663 Liberty Drive
Bloomington, IN 47403
www.westbowpress.com
1 (866) 928-1240

Because of the dynamic nature of the Internet, any web addresses or links contained in this book may have changed since publication and may no longer be valid. The views expressed in this work are solely those of the author and do not necessarily reflect the views of the publisher, and the publisher hereby disclaims any responsibility for them.

Any people depicted in stock imagery provided by Getty Images are models, and such images are being used for illustrative purposes only. Certain stock imagery © Getty Images.

ISBN: 978-1-9736-6320-1 (sc)
ISBN: 978-1-9736-6322-5 (hc)
ISBN: 978-1-9736-6321-8 (e)

Library of Congress Control Number: 2019906560

Print information available on the last page.

WestBow Press rev. date: 07/08/2019

"The greatest legacy one can pass on to one's children and grandchildren is not money or other material things accumulated in one's life. But rather a legacy of character and faith." *Billy Graham*

In Gratitude

I would like to thank my daughter, Cindy McKeowen, for being my editor throughout this venture to take a dream and transform it into a reality. We spent many afternoons reflecting on family memories, revising documents, and preparing this manuscript for print. Your dedication to seeing our story made available to others will always be a treasure in my heart! Also, a sincere note of gratitude to my daughter, Polly Fitzgibbon, for reading my working copy and offering her valuable insight.

To each of our children, what an honor to be your mom! You demonstrated unconditional love as we grew together during the early years. My heart is bursting with pride in how you've matured, and continue to make a positive impact in the world around you. You are my children, and now my friends. Oh, how I love you!

All of this would not be possible without my husband, Linnie. Thank you for the first phone call so many years ago, and for always asking, "Are you okay?" For saying "you're beautiful" first thing in the morning, and always being our family rock. Thank you for your patience when I sat for hours at the computer writing and rewriting text. I love you, Babe.

A note of thanks to Westbow Press throughout the publishing process. Thank you for upholding Christian standards, and for your advice and encouragement.

Most of all, I want to give thanks to my Lord and Savior, Jesus Christ. Lord, you planted this dream in my heart years ago and would not let me rest until our family experiences were translated onto paper. I pray this story blesses many.

And to couples who are embracing the many challenges of a blended family, hang in there. The best is yet to come.

Annette B. Sutcliffe

Contents

PART 3

INTRODUCTION

I first met Michelle in our bank in Orangeburg, SC where Linnie and I were checking on our VISA card. We were making conversation during the visit when I asked her about her family.

"Michelle, how many kids do you and your husband have?" I asked.

"We have four between us," she answered shyly. "He has two and I have two. But right now my husband and I are separated."

"Oh no, that's too bad!" I exclaimed. "Putting two families together is not an easy task. Linnie and I put two families together forty-six years ago, and with God's help and encouragement, we made it work. You know, Michelle, when two people come together to make a home, it's hard, and when six or eight or ten come together to make a home, it is three times as hard. I wish you would reconsider and get your husband to agree to go to a Christian counselor to help you in putting your new family back together."

"Mrs. Sutcliffe, I just think it may be too late for us. I tried and tried, but I just couldn't make it work.

"Linnie and I had the odds stacked against us when we married in 1973. He had five children and I had three. All of our families said it probably wouldn't work. But with our faith in Christ, constant prayer, and our determination to prove everyone wrong, we made it work. Linnie and I promised each other that we would both treat all of the kids as our own and never show partiality."

Time was about up for our visit and I asked Michelle, "Would you mind if I encourage you from time to time in your quest for a

Christ-centered marriage?" She immediately agreed and gave me her business card. Michelle took a pen and quickly wrote her address and phone number on the back. "And Michelle, I will commit to pray for you and your family every day. Let's just see what God will do with this problem!"

I began to send Michelle cards and notes each week or so, and I prayed for her family every day. I stopped by the bank one day and gave her a copy of my cookbook which I published in 2012 as South Carolina 2010 Mother of the Year. A few months later, I received the following note from her:

"Hey, Mrs. Sutcliffe, I was so glad to get your note the other day and to hear that you are writing a book. You will be happy to hear that our family is back together and doing well. We are still in counseling but everything is going great. We are having the family altar every night when we can pray together. We are also back in church. Please continue to remember our family and especially our four kids in your prayers. Love, Michelle."

Holding the note in my hands, I repeated over and over "Praise the Lord. Praise the Lord. Praise the Lord." Linnie walked in and said, "What is going on?"

"It's Michelle, from the bank. Don't you remember? I just opened up this note from her. Let me read it to you."

I read the note to Linnie, and stopped several times to wipe the tears from my eyes. Linnie smiled at me, and said, "Well, how about that?"

"I have to admit. I didn't think God would move so fast!" I said. "I tell you, I am continually amazed at the power of prayer and how God moves in amazing ways."

Most second marriages with children involved end up in the divorce courts. Linnie and I have beaten the odds by keeping our family together with God's help and His blessing. And we had fun in the process.

Over the years I have counseled several couples in second marriages who were having major problems, especially where children were involved. Each time, I shared with these couples how Linnie and I always sought God for wisdom and direction in our family. With every decision. This is exactly how I encouraged, prayed for, and counseled Michelle. Reading her note made my heart sing. And I wanted to share my heart's cry to other families. To know and experience hope. To have a family with God, for God, and honoring God.

So, here's my story. This book gives you an inside look at the Sutcliffe family doing it God's way!

PART 1

Chapter 1

WHAT A LIFE

All through grade school, I was shy – so shy, in fact, I would rarely speak in class. It made for good conduct grades but was bad for a healthy self-image. I remember in the second grade a boy teasing me so badly that I cried all the way home and didn't want to go back to school the next day. In the seventh grade my teacher called me Louise for three weeks until a classmate told her my name was Annette. She apologized, I blushed, and everybody laughed. It seemed like everybody was always laughing. By the time I reached high school, my reputation went with me - "bashful Brunson." By this time I was convinced of my complete insufficiency in everything I attempted.

I did all the things normal teen-agers do—struggled to get good grades, dated, even mustered enough courage to try for majorette in the high school band (and made it), and actually got a part in our senior opera in glee club. I attended Sunday school and church and was fairly active in our youth fellowship at church; but despite the encouragement from friends and the awards received during high school, I began college with the same low self-esteem that had beset me thus far. I actually had a fear of meeting new people or speaking before strangers but managed to hide this feeling from most of my friends.

I joined the church when I was twelve but did not know Jesus as my Savior and Lord. It seemed to be what all my friends were doing.

God did not become real to me until I was eighteen years old. I was attending a youth retreat with the church, my purpose for going being just to "have a good time." After "playing around" during most of the retreat (even skipping several classes) I participated in a candlelight service which was to conclude the retreat. Suddenly sensing Christ's presence as never before, I accepted Him as my Lord and Savior, asking His forgiveness for my sins.

I don't know if it was because Christ was now Lord of my life, but sometime during my first year of college I began to take a deeper look at "me", a person created by God, a unique individual, in His image, and with distinct traits and abilities. Why was I constantly "putting myself down" when in fact I was a very special person to God? When my mind was made up to like myself, just the way I was, my personality glowed with an exhilarating newness, and I began to gain confidence in myself like never before.

After one year of college, I married my high school sweetheart, Ed Carter, against my parents' wishes. At eighteen I thought I knew just about everything I needed to know for starting a life of my own.

Wow! Knowledgeable and wise I was not! My husband-to-be had just started a new job, we had no money saved, and we had to borrow what we needed to buy furniture for our small apartment. With no pre-marital counseling (which should be a "must" for two people considering a life-long commitment), we embarked on what I believed to be a beautiful "lived happily ever after" romance. I wish I could say we 'lived happily ever after'. I wish I could say everything was beautiful - - but it wasn't. When the wedding bells stopped, the bills started. Bills we never considered began to come in, and it became a struggle to pay them. I don't advocate the necessity of being wealthy to be happy. Many couples I know married with less, struggled together, and with God's help, had a happy, successful marriage. My failure, first, was neglecting to seek God for direction, and then attempting to build a successful relationship in my own strength. My immaturity, coupled with my husband's nature, magnified by our failure to dedicate our commitment to God and make Him the center of our home, caused us many times of hurt and disappointment. I loved my husband, Ed, deeply and he loved me; but a marriage requires more than that. I was either too young, too immature, too ignorant or a combination of all three to understand that.

Twelve years and three children later, we were still together after three trial separations. Still together after many fights, and countless periods of soul-searching and rededication to each other. I daresay if I had "let go and let God", or allowed the Holy Spirit to fill and dominate my life, things would have been quite different. But I didn't. I selfishly maneuvered in my own power, trying to manipulate my husband at the same time with my nagging, badgering, pouting and temper tantrums.

Regrets? Yes, I have some. I regret the years I blundered without seeking God's will. I regret the years I wasted not being a productive servant for Him. Oh, yes, we were both born-again Christians. We attended church. We gave to God's work – sometimes. We made feeble attempts to come back to Christ, crying out when we were in trouble or distress.

I don't regret the twelve years of marriage. There were countless happy times that seem to somehow overshadow the sad ones. The miracle is that now I remember the good times so much clearer than the bad. I have three beautiful children who have created wonderful memories from those years. Three weeks before Ed's death, he was in the hospital for tests. He asked me one day when I was with him if we could both rededicate ourselves and our marriage to God. Together we read God's Word and prayed, something we hadn't done together very often. When I got home, I prayed again, asking God to come into our home and marriage and also to remold us and conform us both to His will. Those last three weeks were the happiest of my marriage. And then Ed had a tragic car accident which took his life. Why did God choose to take Ed at a time when the clouds seemed to be lifting and the rainbow in sight? I've asked myself that many times. I still don't have an answer. But I do know that Ed was within God's will when he was killed and that's enough for me.

When I accepted the finality of his death, I began to pick up the pieces of my life and start building anew. I can't say there was no bitterness or doubt. There was. I cried out to God. And I knew God understood, because Jesus wept, grieving his friend, Lazarus's death. (John 11:35) I asked "Why me, Lord?" many times during the first months of widowhood, which is such a natural response to death and grieving. He sustained and comforted me when I experienced periods of extreme loneliness and desperation.

Then, after four years of struggling through widowhood, searching for happiness I sometimes felt had eluded me, I embarked on a new career, a new adventure, that of being a Proverbs 31 wife in a Christ-controlled marriage. What a difference!

And now a new chapter in my life had begun. It began when God allowed a certain man to ask me to become his wife and help him make a home for eight wonderful children. It has continued as we have all grown together in our love for each other and love for God. It is a continuing journey because of the joy and happiness I am experiencing in my life. Sure, I still hurt sometimes, cry sometimes, and still may experience a bit of depression sometimes. Who doesn't? But overshadowing the negative feelings are the positive. I feel complete peace. I feel total joy and contentment, no matter what crisis I must face. That's the great challenge and joy of being a wife and mother. To work, pray, and leave the rest to God. And He makes no mistakes!

Chapter 2

HERE WE ARE

I f somebody had told me I would be facing nine people at the
breakfast table every morning, I'd have said, "You're crazy!"
Never in my wildest fantasies could I have conjured up anything
as preposterous as living with nine other people under one roof.

I never even considered having a large family; three children
were quite enough. Then, six wonderful people slipped into my life
and before I realized what was happening, I had fallen in love with
all of them.

This is my story of how God worked in and through the lives
of ten people to bring an "impossible dream" into reality. It is the
story of each of those ten people, and it is with their permission and
blessing that I reveal the joys, sorrows, traumas and just plain fun
that touched our lives since two families became one. With God's
help, we made it work.

I'd like to introduce you to each member of our team (we always
operate as a team) as they were when Linnie and I first got married
in 1973.

First, there's Linnie, Jr., "Lin" a tall, handsome, eighteen-year-
old first born son who follows in his dad's shadow – considerate,
kind, always thinking of others first. Quick witted and quiet, Lin
loves to work out, and has the muscles to show for it. He can be
found many evenings on the den floor with thousands of Lego
blocks, designing and constructing buildings, vehicles, and other

imaginative structures. Lin spent a large portion of one summer trimming a nearby ditch of chinaberry trees. Drenched with sweat, but loving every moment of being outside, Lin took pride in working to complete a task. Lin was also employed at a local grocery store as a meat cutter. Lin began Clemson University the fall after I came to Norway and became his mom.

Next comes Thea – seventeen with a very positive outlook on life. On any given day, we hear Thea's laughter resonating throughout the house. It is contagious! With dark brown hair and glasses, Thea is a voracious reader. She walks around from room to room with a book in hand, reading as she prepares meals, does chores, or enjoys a snack. Thea is posed to enter Orangeburg-Calhoun Technical College's Medical Laboratory Technician Program after she completes high school. Thea is an excellent student, and committed to her chosen field. She has a wonderful personality and is very easy going.

Following Thea is Polly – fifteen and wise beyond her years. She is 5' 2", with long, silky brown hair and fair skin. Polly has the "patience of Job" most of the time and acts as mediator when the kids have disagreements. She is always the "spokesman" for the group when they had a special request for Mom and Dad. Polly used to have a hard time keeping her dates straight, while she had so many vying for her attention. When she was still in high school, Polly had a habit of forgetting to tell us when she had a date. Since we always required that the kids let us know in advance of their plans, she was chastised on several occasions. One Thursday at work I took my lunch out, prepared to eat, and written on my boiled egg in red ink were these words, "Mom, I have a date Friday night. Hope it's okay. Polly".

Eddie follows Polly, being two months younger and very reluctant to admit the difference in ages. With blonde hair, an athletic build, and good looks, Eddie loves drawing, painting, and is preparing for a career in architecture. Eddie takes pride in his grades and especially excels in math. (He even taught his teacher in geometry class!) He loves to play tennis but hates to shell beans during vegetable season. Except for sleeping in a bed for seven days without making it and having a strange taste for a sloppy room (says he can't find anything if the room is clean), he is a source of joy to all of us. One summer while playing basketball, Eddie injured his knee and underwent surgery, rendering him unable to work or bear weight during his recovery. Eddie painted numerous projects while he was recovering, and had an art show in our home. Many friends and family came to purchase his paintings in support of Eddie's efforts to save money that summer.

Julie, twelve years old with dark, beautiful hair and a twinkle in her eyes, always embraces hard work with vigor and tenacity. Julie loves the outdoors and enjoys working in the flower garden with our many roses. She can be found most days, donned in overalls, helping her dad bale hay or driving the tractor. Julie's love for horticulture has led her to work in a local florist where she learned to arrange live, dried, and an assortment of flowers and greenery to make beautiful displays. Julie is our Christmas "sneak". She spent the days before Christmases searching in closets for hidden gifts, too excited to wait until Christmas morning!

With long brown hair mingled with blonde highlights, Cindy, an eleven year old preteen, shares a room with Julie. Shy and artistic, she can melt your heart with a smile –if you are lucky enough to see one while she sports a mouthful of braces. Cindy loves to cook, sew, and make biscuits which her two brothers rave about. She hates to work outdoors, says it's "not work for a girl", but pitches in anyway. She makes many of her clothes and really does a professional job! She inherited my temperament to a degree, quiet and sensitive, (many times too sensitive) but always seeks the Lord for direction in her life. She always complained that God didn't give her a talent, that she couldn't do anything. One day she picked up the guitar I had given her years before and has been playing beautifully ever since. On any given day you can hear Cindy in her room, playing the guitar and singing songs she's written and composed. Cindy often declares, "It is NOT easy being a girl!" (Well said, Cindy!)

Mark, our nine-year-old, is blonde, intelligent, and has endless energy. He is willing to tackle any job, no matter how hard. One spring just before planting season Linnie suffered a ruptured disc which required back surgery. While Linnie recovered in the hospital, Mark drove the tractor every day after school until all sixty acres of our land were plowed. We were immensely proud. Mark, diagnosed with ADHD at an early age has had to learn how to channel his energy, manage impulsiveness, and focus on a task. A student in the third grade, Mark was performing below grade level. However, doctors at Duke University where Mark was tested, informed me of his ability to accomplish fifth grade work. Extremely meticulous about his room and appearance, Mark is uncompromising on detail and order. One day the kids let our dog in the house. Well, the dog somehow found his way into Mark's room. I walked by later and found Mark on his hands and knees picking the dog hairs out of his carpet, fussing under his breath! Short in stature, I often found Mark hanging by his arms from the clothesline, trying to get taller. Mark can always make us laugh.

With short, dark hair, an olive complexion that darkens beautifully in the summer sun, and a quiet temperament, Janet is nine and the youngest of our children. The outdoor type – Janet loves to wear old jeans, a straw hat and spend hours in the yard, by the creek, or in a nearby field. Janet is a finicky eater, and is often the last to leave the table, pushing food around her plate. Janet never asks for much. She is always just content with what she has, and makes the most out of any situation.

In addition to these eight wonderful children is Linnie, Sr. - my husband, lover, friend, and stalwart father through and through. Tall, handsome, strong, and a man of faith, he has always been God's ordained head of our home. Always in command, and a figure of authority, Linnie chartered new waters as father to eight and never faltered. And underneath that authoritative image is hidden a warm, sincere individual who, though he would never admit it, is very vulnerable when it comes to his family. On one occasion, Linnie won a safety suggestion award of $200 from his employer, Carolina Eastman. After giving a tithe to our church, he divided the rest between the children and me, refusing to keep any for himself. Linnie is a man who does everything right - - well, almost everything. I'll always remember the night at the supper table when he suddenly realized that he had forgotten to fill the car with gas, after having cautioned all of us two days before, "Never leave a car on empty." Needless to say, all eight children gathered around the table, stifled their laughter as I mused, "That's all right, Daddy, nobody's perfect." One day Linnie bought a new bucket to keep under the tractor shed and told everyone to be very careful with it. Two weeks later on a Saturday morning he sheepishly confessed to me that he had backed over it with the tractor. At the supper table that night Mark asked, "What happened to the new bucket? It's all bent on one side." I smiled, turned slowly toward Linnie, who rarely wanted to admit a mistake, and said, "Daddy, everyone would like to know what happened to your new bucket. It's all bent on one side. Would you happened to know?" Of course Linnie had to confess, and the entire family finally burst into laughter.

This is our family – and as our story unfolds I hope that you will come to know each one and understand that it was not an "impossible dream" to put these families together, but truly a "great adventure."

Chapter 3

THE MEETING

Flinging my arms wildly in the dark, I groped for the ringing alarm clock by the bed. "It should be against the law for anyone to get up before daylight," I thought, as I forced my eyes open. I could hear Eddie in the kitchen cooking breakfast.

"I should be thankful. Not many mothers have a son who, at fourteen, will cook, babysit, or do anything else needed around the house. Not many mothers are as blessed as I am with three good kids. Then why am I not joyous, thankful, and happy this glorious morning? It's two weeks before Christmas, the season to be jolly. What's the matter with me?"

I had been trying to shake this feeling for days. Everyone at the office was excited about Christmas shopping, parties, the holidays, but I couldn't seem to "get into the Christmas spirit." Every year since Ed had died in a terrible car accident, I sank into an emotional valley around Thanksgiving which sometimes lasted until after the new year. Every year I thought it would be easier, but every year was the same.

As the season approached and people at work began to talk of going home for the holidays and getting together as couples, a feeling of severe loneliness would engulf me.

"But you've got your kids," well-meaning friends would say. "Be thankful." Sure I was thankful for my kids - - thankful that they weren't in the car with their dad when it veered out of control and struck the tree. Thankful they had adjusted to his death. But the emotional valley was still there every year, and this Christmas season hadn't proved different from the past three. Widowhood for me had not been easy. The depression of the first year, adapting to a new life, and learning to make all decisions concerning the children had been a tremendous struggle. After dating for almost two years, I'd become discouraged at the prospect of ever marrying again, determined not to enter into a permanent relationship simply to cure my loneliness.

My thoughts were interrupted by Mark's crying. I slipped quickly into my robe and hurried out of the bedroom, to find Mark and Cindy pulling at each other in the hall.

"He won't leave my things alone!"

Cindy tried to be calm, but it was evident by the irritation in her voice that her patience was spent. At eleven, she was already very particular about her room and private possessions. Mark was inevitably intruding upon her privacy, and now she was openly resenting it. I wearily separated them and told Cindy to finish dressing, assuring her it wouldn't happen again. I took Mark into my room for a "talk." I was reluctant to spank him again, even though he had thrown his fists at Cindy in full force. As I dried his tears, I prayed that I would do the right thing, say the right thing. Mark had recently been diagnosed at Duke University with hyper kinesis. Mark's impulsive behavior was compounded by the intense grief he felt after Ed's death. All of the doctors emphasized that I would need to exercise added understanding and individualized care for Mark, especially during this time. I wanted desperately to undo some of the damage I had already done in the way I had disciplined Mark in the past.

"But Momma, everybody has a room but me. I got nowhere to put my toys!" He was sobbing again, partly from fear of another spanking and partly to play on my sympathy, an art he had learned quite early.

"I know, Mark, but I'm doing the best I can. You'll have to share a room with Eddie for now, until I can get a bigger house."

It was always the same argument, the same problem. The exceptional child, the demanding child, needs a room of his own. The experts could say that, but the experts didn't make the house payments. I chastised Mark for lashing out at Cindy, trying vainly to explain how bad it was for him to lose his temper. How much could his confused, nine-year-old mind understand? It hadn't been many weeks ago that he threw a lawn chair at Cindy in the yard because he was angry at her.

I pulled him close to me on the bed, placed my arms around his drooping shoulders, and gently kissed his tear-stained cheek.

"Mark, I want you to know I love you very much, but you have to control your temper. If you do lose your temper, there will be consequences. Because of your behavior this morning, there will be no television for several days."

I could feel his small shoulders sag even more under my arm. I dried his swollen eyes, kissed him again, and sent him to his room to get dressed for school.

By the time I got lunches packed, dishes cleaned up, and left for work, I wondered how I'd make it through the day. "Being a working mother is hard," I thought, as I fought the morning traffic. "But being a working mother, father, and provider is almost impossible." I stopped for a traffic light and glanced across the street at the bank on the corner. It was gaily decorated with Christmas reds and greens, almost like a giant Christmas package, complete with bows. I resolved to make this a happy Christmas for the children, even though it may be a lonely one for me. All of my friends had been trying to get me out of the slump by finding eligible men for me to date, but it never seemed to work out. I had almost decided not to date anymore for a while. Then my sister-in-law, Sandra Elkins, called and told me about a nice friend she wanted me to meet.

"If you'll just agree to have coffee with him. Then judge for yourself."

"I just don't feel like it's any use, Sandra."

"Look, Annette, it's not a lifelong commitment. Just one coffee date. I'll tell him to call you tomorrow at work. Is that okay?"

I wasn't at all anticipating the start of another friendship but didn't feel like arguing, either. So I agreed to see him. By this time I was a little curious about Linnie Sutcliffe. Sandra piqued my interest as she painted an almost unreal picture of this friend. He was in his late thirties, tall, good-looking, non-drinker, non-smoker, loved the Lord, and was divorced.

"What more could a girl ask for?"

"Maybe he lost my telephone number," I mused. As I drove into the parking lot at the office, my mind quickly shifted to the top basket on my desk which was crammed with overdue work. By 3:30 p.m. exhaustion began to close in. I had long ago forgotten the expected call. So, when I heard a masculine voice introducing himself on the phone, I was momentarily taken back.

"Sutcliffe – Linnie Sutcliffe. Sandra tells me you may be interested in having coffee with me one night. How about this Friday about 7:30?"

"Okay. I hope you don't mind entertaining three kids, because I don't have a sitter. I'll see you Friday." After quickly giving him directions to my house, I hung up, wondering if I had made a mistake.

The moment the receiver rested on the hook, my reservations about this man and this whole idea began to multiply. "There just has to be something wrong with him," I thought. His attributes were simply too good to be true. It was the Friday before Christmas, 1972, when that "something" became evident!

My date arrived right on time, in the midst of the excitement my three children displayed over a new "suiter" for momma. Mark greeted him first.

"Hey! I'm Mark. Are you gonna be my new Daddy?"

"Mark!"

I apologized for Mark's frankness as I took my date's coat, soaked from the downpour that had begun. "What a way to begin a new friendship," I thought. Eddie and Cindy were introduced to Linnie and then they all left us to watch their favorite television show in another room. As I checked on the coffee and busied myself in the kitchen, I looked my date over. I was impressed. He was very good looking, tall, with dark hair that glistened at the temples with a touch of grey. Wearing a dark suit and red tie, he looked elegant. I thought, "Wow, does he have good taste in clothes!"

"That coffee smells mighty good," he said as he turned his head in my direction. He flashed me a smile that began to melt the reservations I had harbored for days. He talked easily about his work and his plans for the holidays as we enjoyed coffee. I could sense that this was a very warm, intelligent man who had strong feelings and convictions about his faith and his relationship with Christ. His ease in conversation was contagious and I soon found myself talking of Christmas holidays and my children, really laughing and enjoying myself for the first time in months. Suddenly he reached back for his wallet.

"Would you like to see my family?" He proudly displayed his children's pictures, falling out of his wallet like an accordion.

"There's Linnie, Jr., eighteen. He graduates next June. This is Thea, she's seventeen. Polly, let's see, she must be fourteen. Julie, twelve, and Janet, the baby, she's nine."

As he showed me each photograph, I prayed that the shock I felt inside wasn't apparent. I struggled with my composure as he continued to talk about his kids and how they managed in a one-parent home. My well-meaning sister-in-law, the matchmaker, had given me every detail about this man – except for the five children! Needless to say, the remainder of the evening was a blur, and I bade him goodnight (and good-bye) as quickly as possible without wishing to seem discourteous, feeling that we would never meet again.

At work the following Monday, everyone wanted to know how

my "date" had turned out and they all laughed when I announced that he had a ready-made family.

"This guy is looking for a mother and a maid. I need a lot of things right now, but one thing I don't need is five more kids! No more coffee with that guy – no way."

Every day for the next week I kept telling myself how lucky I was to have had such a narrow escape. He must be crazy to think that I would even consider dating him again with his "family connections." But for some reason my mind would wander back to that Friday night. I asked myself over and over "Why did he have to be so nice, everything I had hoped for and prayed for these last few years?" When Linnie called two weeks later and asked if he could come by again for coffee, my voice said "yes" before my head could say "no."

To this day I don't know why I accepted that second invitation except to acknowledge that God was already at work in both our lives to bring a beautiful plan to fulfillment. I didn't know until much later that Linnie was fighting the same battle with himself, not wanting to get involved. But, at the same time, longing to be able to share his thoughts and dreams with someone who may understand. Neither of us realized that our amazing Lord was taking the loose threads in each of our lives and beautifully and lovingly weaving them together into an unbelievable tapestry.

Chapter 4

THE MAZE

There was no magic feeling, no "love at first sight" between Linnie and me. We were just two people with similar problems who needed companionship. I kept telling myself, "Don't get alarmed, just enjoy his company, his friendship. Just don't get involved – keep it friendly."

One coffee date led to another and before long I found myself eagerly awaiting Linnie's next call. One Saturday morning about four weeks after our first rainy night date, I received a beautiful bouquet of carnations with a simple note, "Thinking of you." I was deeply touched by such thoughtfulness, but tried desperately to remain practical.

"So, what's a few flowers," I rationalized? "He's trying to get to me with flowers, but he doesn't know me very well. It won't do him any good at all!" I tucked the card away in a drawer, for whatever reason I still don't know, and found myself going back to the drawer to read it over and over again.

Linnie's calls became more frequent and, on my part, more and more anticipated. He called one Saturday morning and asked if Mark would like to spend the day at his home. Mark was elated at the prospect, but I was hesitant. I could only imagine that Mark might have difficulty, even for a day, in a very different environment. Between the two of them, I could hardly say "no", so off Mark went for a day in the country. That night a very weary little nine-year-old came running in to fill me in on the day's activities.

"Momma, I had so much fun! I saw his pigs, and we played and Janet and me climbed a tree and can I go again, please?"

The excitement in his voice and ecstatic sparkle in his eyes quickly melted any reservations I felt. Mark eagerly recounted every detail of his day on the farm. When I finally got him calmed down enough to take a bath and get into bed, it didn't take many minutes for him to fall asleep. After Cindy and Eddie were settled for the night, Linnie and I sat and talked of our children, our mutual problems, and the unsettled future. I admitted my sense of failure with Mark and my inability to cope with some situations.

"I love kids", Linnie said warmly. "I'll do anything I can to help Mark."

As the days moved into weeks, Linnie and I saw more and more of each other. Mark began to look forward to his visits with great delight, and it was evident that Cindy and Eddie approved. We had long talks about our tragedies, our children and the multitude of problems involved in a one-parent home. Without realizing it, I was becoming dependent upon his advice and counsel regarding matters in my own home.

In February, 1973, I developed the worst case of flu I'd ever had. It began on Sunday night and all through the week I suffered the typical flu symptoms – high fever, cough, stuffy nose and headache. Linnie called daily and I jumped every time the phone rang, anticipating his calls. On Friday he asked if he could drop by for a few minutes. Eagerly looking forward to his visit, I did not stop to consider that my appearance wasn't very appealing after being confined to bed all week. That afternoon one dozen red carnations arrived with a note, "Maybe this is just what the doctor ordered."

When Linnie arrived, I tried vainly to appear casual and friendly but, not being very good at concealing my feelings, I'm afraid he could clearly see the happiness in my face! He sat by my bed and began to talk in his usual, easy manner. We both made a vain attempt to remain nonchalant as he talked of his work and his kids. I could sense a deep love and devotion to his five children whom he spoke of so often. I greatly admired his confidence in running a home and caring for five children, always displaying assurance and calmness with every situation. I was still fighting the battle of self-control regarding our relationship, struggling not to become involved. We talked briefly and then he leaned forward, and kissed me tenderly before leaving for home.

"I'll miss you", he said. And he was gone. Unable to sleep, I began to relive the past two months in my life and the changes that had transpired. What had been a day-by-day existence for me had transformed into a marvelous adventure. This man with whom I did not wish to become involved had become centermost in my life. My days had become a prelude to the visits and coffee in the evenings. Slowly, I realized that I had ceased to think of Linnie Sutcliffe, the father of five, and had begun to fall in love with Linnie Sutcliffe, the man. As the reality of my feelings slowly sank in, a pang of panic struck. He had never implied any interest in me other than friendly concern. He never made any commitment throughout the past months, except to say he missed me when we were apart. How did I know he didn't want "just friendly conversation", not wishing to get tied down with a serious commitment? Hadn't he, in fact, stated the first night that it would be a long time before he would commit himself to another woman? It was with mixed emotions that sleep finally came.

After several weeks passed, Linnie surprised me one day with the proposal to meet his children. I felt a mixture of apprehension and fear, not knowing how they would receive me. I planned a hamburger cookout in my yard with some friends so that a possibly tense situation might be avoided. I had only met these children through pictures and Linnie's loving description of each one. He talked endlessly about each child when we were together.

When they arrived, my apprehension quickly dissolved as my heart went out to each of them. They were shy but well behaved and courteous. As the afternoon wore into evening, their shyness disappeared and we talked of many things-- school, the fast approaching summer vacation, etc. Being one who always loved to study human behavior, I observed each of these five kids and my admiration for their father grew even more. It didn't take long for me to determine that they were completely devoted to their dad and loved and respected him greatly. When they prepared to leave, Julie and Janet, the two youngest, ran up and kissed me on the cheek. I felt I'd really been accepted!

As our dates became closer and the long-distance calls more frequent, I began to sense that Linnie's feelings for me were much deeper. But he never committed himself, or talked about a serious relationship. Then one Saturday, after returning from shopping, I found a beautiful bouquet of flowers on my doorstep with a note which read, "Just had to let you know I love you."

My suspicions were confirmed. We both loved each other, but with an impossible love, one which may never be brought to fulfillment. The questions and doubts began to overshadow my secure world. It was one thing to have a wonderful relationship together as we did and at the same time have the security of a home which was paid for, children who were somewhat adjusted to life without a father, and a secure job. But it was quite another thing to think of stepping into a relationship where there most surely were overwhelming odds.

I had to make a decision regarding our relationship before any question about the future was brought up, because I would do anything to keep from hurting Linnie. For the next week the questions kept haunting me. How could anyone, even us, put ten people together in one house and succeed? Even with our faith in each other, in our children, and in our God, it seemed to be an impossible dream, a dream which becomes a reality only in the make-believe world of television and movies. I had seen many couples with children on both sides marry, only to find after several months that they couldn't make it work. Then followed another tragedy, another divorce, and more heartbreak for the children. Did we have any right to even consider the possibility of a merger of the two families with eight children involved? What repercussions would follow such a union?

What about the wishes of the eight children involved? My three kids would have to be removed from one way of life and placed in an entirely different environment. Adapting to a new town, a new church, and new friends would be easy for me, but could I say the same for my children? Did I have the right to even ask this of them? They were secure in their schools, were reasonably happy and adjusted, and were blessed with material things. Would they accept this change without bitterness and resentment? Would they accept another man in the place of their father? And what about Linnie's five children? Maybe they were satisfied with life as it was. After emerging from the tragedy of a broken home, they were probably reasonably well adjusted and happy. But, what kind of scars would they possibly have? They seemed to keep their home clean, were very adept at helping Linnie with kitchen chores, washing and ironing and evidently worshipped their father. How would they feel about a stranger coming into their lives and accepting the role they had filled so well? Another question was where could we possibly house a family of ten? Certainly not at Linnie's home with only four bedrooms. And definitely not at mine where I had only three.

The questions were endless. There were weeks of searching and prayer on my part since I wanted what God wanted for all of us. I did not want selfishness to mar my thinking. We were not only two people, considering a new relationship. We were ten people to be considered individually, and then collectively. The more I prayed the more convinced I became that this venture would work. As doubt gave way to assurance and I began to feel the reality of God's presence and his peace, the odds didn't seem so great, the problems not so insurmountable.

I realized that even if Linnie and I did decide to enter into a permanent relationship, the problems wouldn't disappear. There would be terrific adjustments for all the children, as well as for us. Our lives as a blended family would no doubt have to navigate many turns and bends in the road. I've never expected God to remove all the obstacles from our paths, for it is through encountering obstacles that we become better able to cope with life and become closer in our walk with Jesus Christ. But, after experiencing this great adventure for over forty-five years, I can say from experience and based on the authority of the bible that God makes no mistakes. We have indeed faced a maze of dilemmas and strife. But through it all, God prevailed. And we held fast to God, turning to Him in every struggle for wisdom and direction. I attribute the success we have encountered not to our efforts alone, but to God's constant guidance. Yeah, every maze brought us right back to Him!

Chapter 5

THE MERGER

More and more Linnie talked of the future when we were together, always being careful never to commit himself, but I began to sense that he was subtly including the children and me in his plans. We had discussed our feelings for each other many times, but the subject of marriage was never mentioned.

One night we were sitting in my den, quietly talking of the past loneliness we had both felt, the traumas we had both experienced, when the conversation drifted to the future. "What about the future" I thought, a little annoyed. "He keeps talking about <u>our</u> future someday, and has never asked how I feel about the matter." My thoughts were suddenly interrupted by the words " . . . when I . . ." I listened a little closer to his words, . . . can add a room on the house for Mark."

"Now, wait a minute." I spoke rather sharply. He was astonished, but I continued, "You are making a great deal of plans – and assumptions. Don't you think you'd better ask if I want to spend the rest of my life in that house before you plan to add a room for Mark?"

"Oh, Annette, you don't understand. I've wanted to ask you to be my wife. You don't know how badly I've wanted to. I just didn't think I had the right to ask you to give up so much security to take on another family – to take such a gamble on the future. I love you with all my heart, but I don't want to be selfish either. I don't have a lot of money. We'd have a struggle, that's for sure. I was so afraid you may not want to give up what you have here."

"You wonderful, crazy, adorable man", I exclaimed as I threw my arms around his neck. "Yes, I do want to be your wife if you think we can make this marriage work. I think, with God's help, we can."

The rest of the evening was spent making plans, talking endlessly about the big decisions facing us, and just being happy! We decided to add two rooms and a large den on Linnie's home to make room for our enlarging family. Every detail seemingly "worked itself out" as we sat for hours talking of our new life together. We set the date of our wedding in June because of Linnie's vacation. It would give us two months in which to get the house ready. When we said goodnight, we were two very relieved and very happy people, committed to a life which, to many people, would be an impossible dream but to us was the answer to many prayers.

Several nights later Linnie and I were riding around town. Both of us were quiet for some time and he suddenly reached over and touched my hand.

"Penny for your thoughts."

"Oh, I guess I'm just in a pensive mood tonight, reflecting on what my life has been, dreaming of what it's going to be. No special thoughts. Why?"

"Would you like to see the house?"

With only a moment's hesitation I told him I would. Throughout the 30-minute drive, I was mostly silent, trying to imagine what this home was like. Before this minute I'd not even entertained the possibility of my not liking the house. All Linnie had told me was that it was four years old, brick, with four bedrooms, two baths. What if I didn't like it? Every wife wants to design and decorate her own home. What kind of furnishings did this family like? Would I find it clean? The questions kept invading my mind, and I was deep in thought when I heard Linnie speaking.

"The kids have gone skating, and you may find the house a bit messy," he said as we drove into the yard.

From the moment I stepped through the back door, I fell in love with my new home. My eyes quickly scanned the kitchen and fell on the dining table, a beautiful antique oak which Linnie said had belonged to his grandfather. He had refinished it and placed it in the dining area where it was a perfect fit. And, to my amazement and joy, it was made to seat ten people! As we walked from room to room I marveled at the cleanliness of a home which had been run without a woman for several years. He then showed me where we would add on to the house. As we prepared to leave, Linnie caught my hand.

"Sweetheart, this is your home now. You can furnish it as you like and make any changes you see are needed."

Happiness surged in me. "Oh, Linnie we're going to be truly happy here! I just know it. God has really blessed us. What about the kids? When should we tell them?"

"What's wrong with Saturday night. I'm off for the weekend and we can cook some bar-b-que chickens on the grill and get everybody together and drop our news."

As we walked out and Linnie turned the lock, I thought, "Four years ago I felt as if my life was over. Now I feel like the Lord is drawing back the curtain on a new beginning. Oh, thank you, Lord, for being a prayer-answering God."

We hadn't considered the possibility of one or two out of the eight children resenting this decision we had made. It seemed so completely right, somehow, we just knew they would all be as happy as we were. After a delicious supper and the dishes were done, Linnie gathered all of them around the table. I thought I detected a glint in Eddie's eyes and several of them were grinning. When Linnie told them of our plans, Linnie, Jr., was the first to speak.

"We all sorta figured out what you two had in mind, and we're all for it."

My already joyous heart overflowed as I observed eight smiling faces around that table. It was one of those rare moments that one wants to store in the heart and keep reliving over and over. That experience was the first of many wonderful moments that I would discover in the months and years ahead.

During the last weeks before the wedding, we spent each Saturday together, all ten of us, helping with the house, making final arrangements, and just "getting acquainted." The assurance I felt in my heart that this union was blessed by God as well as the marvelous way all of the kids seemed to get along together, wiped away the warnings of many well-meaning friends who told us that it would never work. "I'd think a long time before stepping into a job like that" or "It's impossible to put ten people under one roof and have peace" are a sample of the advice I received. Sometimes now in recalling those weeks, I wonder why there were never any doubts or hesitation. It was as if God just told me, "This is right" and I went from there.

The day of our wedding dawned beautiful and fair. I awoke as I had each morning for weeks, wondering if this was really happening to me. There was little time for musing for there were many last-minute errands to run. There were the flowers to pick up at the florist, deliveries of several corsages to be made, a "very important" trip to the hairdresser, to name just a few. We had planned a very small ceremony with only our immediate families. My parents had insisted on giving us a small reception at their home. My dear mother-in-law from my previous marriage, who was a widow, was also there to wish us well as was most of my first husband's family. It meant a great deal to me that they were also giving their blessing to this union.

After being late to the church because of a last-minute phone call from someone wishing us best wishes, I walked assuredly down the aisle on my dad's arm to meet Linnie. We faced each other and in a spirit of deep love repeated the wedding vows, promising God and the world to honor and cherish each other until death should part us.

After greeting many friends and enjoying refreshments at the reception, we changed into our travel clothes, gave all of the children last-minute instructions, and said our goodbyes. My three children were staying in Orangeburg with my folks and Linnie's five were staying with his parents in Norway while we enjoyed five glorious days of Florida sun. The memory of those eight telling us goodbye and to have fun was another gem of memory to be stored away in my heart.

Later, while traveling to our honeymoon destination, I said, "You know, we really have an enormous job ahead of us, making a home for my three and your five childre....I mean our eight children." "Having a few doubts?" Linnie smiled, as he squeezed my hand. "I think you know me better than that, Linnie, I responded. It's really going to be an adventure." I couldn't possibly realize as I settled back to enjoy our drive how tremendous the adventure would really be.

Chapter 6

A New Beginning

Every good thing must come to an end, even vacations and honeymoons. Monday found Linnie and me back at our jobs, leaving much of the responsibilities of running the house to the kids. After the first few "hectic days" of adjusting, we sat down and tried to divide the work load. Both of the older boys were working to save for college, and they were excluded from most of the household chores. Lin had been working for two years in a local grocery store when he could, and Eddie had gotten a summer job at the cucumber shed, grading and boxing cucumbers. The hours were long, and the work hard, but he didn't seem to mind after they placed that first paycheck in his hand.

Lin had already been accepted to Clemson University and knew he had to pay for most of his expenses. He had the first semester's tuition paid and was working toward the second. Eddie was determined to go to college but hadn't made up his mind where he wanted to go. I established a savings account for Eddie when he was small, and he began to add to it each week after getting paid. Eddie still had three years to save, and I encouraged him to put as much as he could aside for his education. After working all day, sometimes until 10:00 p.m., neither of them could be expected to do much around the house. That is, except when Lin and Eddie sat down to eat at night consuming what I thought was enough to feed four people. I remember the boys drinking two quarts of orange juice at one sitting. The temperature climbed into the upper 90's many days, and after working in the heat all day, both of them had insatiable appetites.

Linnie and I tried as best we could to be fair and equal with the chores. Until school started and cucumber season was over, Lin and Eddie were given a reprieve. Janet, being only nine, inherited the job of emptying the kitchen trash each afternoon and gathering all trash in the house on Saturday. Mark's job was feeding the pets. As if we didn't have enough mouths to feed, we were the parents of a menagerie of domesticated animals – a cat that was never called anything but "the cat" who somehow sensed my intense dislike of the entire feline breed, seemed to be forever increasing her family in the barn, under the house, or any other unlikely place. She had an uncanny way of appearing at the back screen door at the precise moment we bowed our heads for grace at every meal and would proceed to climb the screen, crying and whining. We finally cured her of that obnoxious habit. Lin got up one day from his place, filled a glass with water, and threw it through the screen, sending her flying down the steps. Thereafter, the kids took turns. After several days, she learned that when one of them arose from the table, she'd better run for her life!

The only productive thing I ever saw "the cat" do (besides get pregnant) was catch mice. It was a common sight to see her marching triumphantly across the back yard, carrying another meal to her lair. By the time we managed to find a good home for the last kitten in a litter, one of the kids would come in say with a note of despair, "Mom, I'm afraid "the cat" is pregnant again!" And the vicious cycle would continue. "The cat" remained with us for three years and then undoubtedly decided it was time to seek greener pastures, because we never saw her again. I'm sure all the kids were convinced I "did away with her" because they gave me funny looks every time someone asked about what could have happened to her. They'll never believe it but I had really grown quite fond of the ole' girl and missed seeing her perched on her favorite spot—atop the sill outside the kitchen window.

Mac was the family comic, a Brittany spaniel that determined to make his bed either in the front seat of the car or in my flower beds. He spent his leisure time retrieving tennis balls, cucumbers, tomatoes and any other object he could find that faintly resembled a ball. The maddest I ever got at Mac was the day he trotted triumphantly into the back yard from our vegetable garden carrying one of Linnie's prize tomatoes in his mouth. Playfully, he placed the luscious, red tomato at my feet for a quick game of fetch! While I was chastising him in anything but a calm, quiet tone, the kids were doubled over with laughter.

"Mom, he's just looking for a ball," one of the kids said. As if he sensed my anger at his thievery in the tomato patch, he turned his attention to Linnie's cantaloupes and stripped every single vine!

Following Mac whenever she could muster up the strength was Beauty—a registered English Setter that had already outlived her time. Beauty spent most of the day reclining in the middle of my flower beds basking in the sun. If we were a little late fixing her supper, she would appear at the back steps and begin to howl in an attempt to hurry us along. She still tried to hunt but her senses were going fast. We all felt a tremendous loss when Linnie had to take her away one day not long after our marriage to be put to sleep by the vet.

To add a little flavor to the pack, I brought a Manchester-Chihuahua from my home who spent her time flirting with Mac or fighting with Beauty. When Beauty passed on, Prissy decided to vent her anger on Mac, so they would be friends one minute, arch enemies the next. When I had just about given up on their ability to get along, I looked out the kitchen window one day and they were snuggled together in Mac's favorite spot - my flower bed. These troublesome, irritating, but lovable animals became Mark's wards.

Thea and Polly, being the oldest girls, inherited the kitchen detail. They helped me stack and wash dishes after meals and started preparing the evening meal each day. There were days when I didn't get home until almost 6:00 p.m., and the art of cooking they hadn't yet mastered was learned fast by trial and error method. In fact, everything in our new home was done by trial and error method. All of us, being novices at this "communal living", blundered, floundered, and prayed our way through the first traumatic months of adjustment. Some days we cooked too much, some days we had to allowance everyone to a small helping because we hadn't cooked enough. We all learned quickly the best and easiest way to handle these situations was to laugh together and share what we had.

Julie and Cindy were placed in charge of folding and stacking all clothes which were to be delivered to the bedrooms before I got home from work. I sorted and washed the clothes at night during the week and the next day they were dried, folded, and delivered. I handled the heavy Saturday wash, sorting and distributing the loads with help from the girls. Six sets of linens plus the other clothes made for an enormous amount of clothes to be washed, and on Saturday the den looked like a laundromat with clothes arranged in their individual stacks.

Since we now had six bedrooms, we gave out assignments – Lin and Eddie would share one of the new bedrooms. Julie and Cindy would share the other one. Polly and Thea would still share a bedroom, and Janet would get a room of her own. Then, Mark would get the last bedroom for his own. Several years before, the physicians shared with me when Mark was diagnosed with ADHD that it was imperative that the hyper-active child have his own space. This was another tremendous answer to my prayers at that time in our lives.

Marking our articles of clothing quickly became a necessity. We had four girls wearing the same size panties and socks, two boys wearing the same size underwear and shirts, and Linnie and both of the older boys wearing the same size socks. After about two weeks of arguing over who got Polly's undies and bra or why they gave me Cindy's bikinis, I invested in a black magic marker and passed it around. I went for a doctor's appointment one day and during his examination the doctor unexpectedly displayed a wide grin. "Annette, I don't mean to be nosy, but could I prevail upon you to tell me what the "ABS" means on your undies?" I smiled sheepishly and answered, "If you lived in a house where four girls wore the same size underwear, what would you do?" My doctor chuckled good that day.

When friends visited in our home and Linnie was leisurely relaxing in his favorite chair with his shoes off, I'm sure they always wondered why the white thread was sewn on the toes of his socks. He called it "wardrobe preservation."

Since their summer was passing all too quickly and the thoughts of school loomed ahead, I left the kids in bed in the mornings and slipped off to work, leaving them a note on the kitchen fridge. Linnie hadn't planted a garden that year because of his obligation to get the house renovated and ready for our combined families. So, there was little outside work for them to do. I knew that the greatest privilege I could give them was sleeping in. It also afforded me the opportunity to have my quiet time, time I quickly learned to cherish in a house with nine other people and in a situation where the incessant demands of a large family sometimes caused me to fall from the mountain top of contentment to an emotional valley of fatigue.

Linnie was on rotating shift work and our schedule had to be somewhat "flexible". But, for the most part after the first week we settled down to living what we considered a normal life – normal, but always with surprises, some of them very, nice surprises. Linnie and I had never discussed what the children would call us. While we were dating, his kids called me "Miss Annette" and mine called him "Mr. Linnie." I guess we just felt that somehow the situation would "work itself out" and the results would be right. I had noticed that days after the marriage the girls would avoid addressing me at all, and I began to wonder whether we should bring the matter out in the open. One day as I was coming home from work, I passed Linnie on the road. He waved, tooted the horn, and continued on his way. As I drove into the back yard, I saw Eddie standing on the back steps, evidently having just come home from the cucumber shed, grimy, and covered with sweat. I gathered my packages and got out of the car, exhausted from a strenuous day at the office but determined not to let the tedious pace there affect my most important job, that of wife and mother. I was engrossed in thoughts of supper, dirty clothes, and staying emotionally "fit" when Eddie's voice jarred me.

"Mom, did you pass Daddy on the road? He said to tell you he had to go to town, and would be right back."

There was no hesitation, no shyness in his reference to "Daddy", as if he had always called him that. In a feeble attempt to mask my shock and not wanting to embarrass him, I dropped one of my packages, my heart surging within me.

"Oh, yes, hon, I just passed him. Would you get that package for me and drop it on my bed?"

I hurried in and stopped in the kitchen long enough to check with the girls on how the day went and how supper was progressing. It had been only a moment – a small speck in the span of a day. To Eddie it had been only a simple statement, innocently made, but to me it was a great deal more. It meant acceptance – acceptance of a new life and of a new dad. Several years later I asked him about that day, and he said he never thought of calling Linnie anything else. "You called him 'Daddy', so I just naturally called him that, too," were his words.

It was as if the entire group was waiting for someone to break the ice. The next day Polly passed me in the hall, carrying a stack of old pictures and a worn album. "Momma, I cleaned out some of the drawers in the china cabinet today. Where should I put these pictures?" A warm, secure glow enveloped me, but not wanting to make her feel uneasy, I casually gave her an answer.

In the days that followed, one by one the kids responded in a like manner – all except Lin. Being the oldest, I was convinced it would be impossible for him to call me "Mom", but the problem was that he never called me anything. It suited me fine for him to just call me "Annette" if it was comfortable for him, but he continued to avoid calling me at all. I never let it cause me undue concern, because I was sure that eventually the matter would resolve itself. After all, seven out of eight seemed to be pretty good odds!

Lin had been at Clemson about four or five weeks and we had gotten several letters from him, describing his schedule and telling the kids all about college life.

I was in the yard one afternoon after supper, trying to replant some shrubbery around the house, when Mark stuck his head out the back door.

"Momma, telephone! I think it's Lin."

I dropped the shovel, shook the black dirt from my hands and hurried inside.

Slightly out of breath, I picked up the receiver.

"Hello."

"Momma?"

I must have been hearing things! He couldn't have said what I thought he just said. My heart skipped a beat.

"Hello?" I said again, assured that I had misunderstood.

"Momma, it's Lin. How's everything going?"

"It's fine, just fine, Lin. How's school?"

I was so excited I could hardly speak. He called me "Momma"! No one asked him to. And he couldn't have felt pressured into it! My mind raced. He just did it! After all those weeks of ignoring my name, weeks of my wondering what he wanted to call me, it sounded so natural when he said it.

I felt totally accepted now, by all of them. As if the family was now complete. Somehow, I managed to get through the remainder of the conversation without letting Lin know how his words had shocked me. We talked for a few more minutes and then he hung up. After I had replaced the receiver on the hook, I stood there for a few moments, basking in this new feeling of wholeness, of fulfillment.

"Thank You, Jesus," I whispered aloud. As I bounced down the steps to get back to my planting, I thought to myself, "I don't know how much more happiness I can stand without just bursting!"

Two weeks after we moved in, my brother came over to help install our air conditioning system. All the duct work had been done, but the compressors had to be wired and connected. We had sweltered in what had to be the hottest summer in the history of Norway – 90's and 100's most days – and we were all eagerly anticipating the added convenience of air conditioning. Since it was going to be an all-day job, we invited his whole family to spend the day with us. After getting a late start (my brother was definitely <u>not</u> an early bird), a car horn signaled their arrival and they spilled out of the car, Al, Gail, his wife, four kids, and a pet poodle. Foreseeing a "slightly" confusing and frustrating day, having six extra guests for dinner along with the strain of cleaning, I had prepared an enormous pot of spaghetti sauce. The morning went fairly well except for me spending half of the time trying to locate tools Linnie couldn't put his hands on. Which he was absolutely "positive" someone else, other than himself, had moved from their intended place of storage. At 11:45 a.m., 15 minutes before my intended deadline for lunch, Lin appeared in the kitchen doorway, followed by Mac, Prissy, and "The Cat."

"What's for dinner? I'm starved! Sorry I'm early but my boss asked me if I could take my lunch hour early today."

He slammed the door in Mac's face, climbed over a toy belonging to my nephew, and disappeared around the corner to the bathroom.

"Don't worry about hurrying. I've got an hour."

The phone pealed out, reverberating through my head. Cindy reached for the receiver while I grabbed a pot and quickly filled it with water.

"Mom," Eddie needs a ride home from the cucumber shed for lunch."

"Oh, wow!" This is all I need, everybody wanting to eat at one time. "Lin, please ride to town and pick Eddie up for lunch. By the time you get back, I'll have yours ready."

While Lin was gone, I called Polly and Thea to make tea and get the table ready for lunch. The kids had been playing outside all morning, and I knew they were plenty hungry. I stopped Polly as she was beginning to set plates on the table.

"Polly, let's serve in shifts, buffet style. It'll be a lot easier. Lin and Eddie can eat first along with Daddy and Uncle Al. Then, we can feed the rest, several at a time. Just put the plates over by the stove."

Lin and Eddie walked in just as we were pouring iced tea in their glasses. Eddie resembled a reject from a Salvation Army mission, his face and clothes covered with dirt and sweat, evidence of a hard morning's work outside.

"Wow! It must be 100 degrees out in that sun!" he said, wiping his face with his handkerchief and waving a quick greeting to his aunt Gail who was sitting by the table. "As soon as I wash up, I'll be ready to eat." He walked toward the bathroom, paused for a moment, and said, "Mom, it looks like it's going to be a long day. I may not get through until after dark, but I'm sure someone at the shed will bring me home. Just thought I'd better let you know I may be late."

"Okay, hon. We'll keep you a plate warm." "He looks so tired, so beat," I thought to myself. "Is it really right to require children to work when their youth passes so quickly? Are we being fair to them?" One part of me wanted to tell both the boys, "Quit working, boys, have a good time while you can. There'll be plenty of time for work when you are adults." But that wouldn't really be fair and I knew it. Linnie and I had discussed this issue, along with many others, and we were in agreement. We had both worked when we were teenagers, helping with expenses at home and knew what it meant to buy our own clothes, pay for gas, and help with college expenses. We wanted our children to grow into adulthood, knowing the value of money, realizing what a hard day's work meant, and to have a sound work ethic. I found myself stifling the impulse many times of telling them not to work so hard, and today was no exception. My thoughts were interrupted by Linnie's voice from outside.

"Hey, it's past 12! Let's get some nourishment on the table."

"Come and get it!" I yelled back at him, filling a plate with spaghetti and covering it with sauce. Lin and Eddie were seated, waiting patiently, and Linnie and Al trudged through the kitchen to join them.

"Where in the world did you get that gigantic pot?" Al laughed as he stopped short at the stove. "It looks like something Linnie must have swiped when he had KP in the Air Force. Linnie, I saw a pot just like this at S & S Cafeteria a couple of months ago. You been there lately?" Al laughed and continued on his way through the kitchen, down the hall, and into the bathroom.

An hour later as we washed the last of the dishes, and I was reveling in the fact that dinner had gone smoothly, sixteen people had been fed within the hour, and the kitchen was almost clean once more. The smaller ones had returned to the outside to play, the men had returned to their work, and Gail and I were chatting as I wiped the last crumbs from the table and stove. Suddenly Janet appeared in the doorway, face smudged with dirt, a frown finding its way across her forehead.

"Momma, I'm hungry. When can I eat?"

I stopped in my tracks, staring at her in utter amazement. I couldn't have forgotten to feed one of the children! I wouldn't! Everybody was called, I thought. I couldn't have left Janet out! I looked at Gail, then back at Janet, vainly searching for an explanation. Gail smiled and spoke up, "I think we forgot to feed someone."

"Oh, Janet, I'm so sorry Honey." My arm went quickly around her shoulders, and with my other hand I pulled the loose strands of long hair away from her eyes. "I didn't mean to leave you out, honest. I thought sure we called everyone. Run and wash your face and hands, and I'll fix you some lunch right now."

She broke away from me and ran for the bathroom, a smile replacing the frown she wore a minute before. She seemed to be glad she had been forgotten in the rush because now she was afforded special treatment by being the only one at the table.

I quickly warmed some spaghetti and fixed her a place at the table. After saying grace with Janet, I sank into the nearest chair and sighed wearily. "Oh, well, I guess if nothing worse happens to this family of 10, I should be grateful." And all three of us laughed.

Before Lin had a chance to really get acquainted with his new family, he had to leave for college the middle of August. He was excited over his first taste of real independence, and all of the kids seemed to be on his heels every minute the last few days, checking to see if he had everything packed, offering to help him get his things ready, and generally sharing his enthusiasm. Janet and Mark parked on his bed at every opportunity, fascinated by his description of campus life, dormitories, and classes. This was a "man-of-the world" telling the younger ones what they could expect out of life, and they were drinking in his words, thirsty for a glimpse of what the future held for them.

The day he left there was a mixture of sadness and excitement pervading the house as we felt the ties of dependence beginning to loosen. Linnie and I felt no different that August morning when Lin left. I had already grown close to him in the few weeks we had together, and hated to see him leave so soon. But time has a way of passing all too quickly, and try as I may to erase the thought from my mind, the reality of his leaving stung as he piled his luggage into his car and said goodbye. Watching the car until it was out of sight, waving as long as I could, I realized that the growing away had begun.

Two weeks later school was beginning for the other seven kids, meaning I had to go shopping for school clothes. I sat down with the kids one night and made a list of what everyone had to purchase. We decided on three pairs of jeans and three tops for each one and one pair of school shoes. Eddie offered to take care of his clothes out of his summer money, so on Saturday before school started, Polly, Thea, Julie, Cindy, Janet and I went to town. I ordered most of Mark's clothes from Sears so he stayed at home with Linnie. After trudging from store to store for two or three hours trying to find the best bargains, I managed to please all five of them, and they each proudly carried their purchases. We ended our excursion at a shoe store where an overzealous salesman approached us, smiling broadly and offering his help.

"Good morning, Ma'am. It's a lovely day, isn't it? Do these lovely young ladies need some new shoes? We have new styles that just came in. What kind did you have in mind?"

"Thank you, I need five pairs. One pair for each girl."

His eyes widened in disbelief and after collecting himself, he went about the business of fitting the girls in the styles they chose. I could tell his curiosity was getting the best of him, since so many of the girls looked so near each other in age. After the last pair had been fitted and I walked to the counter to pay, he took my money, handed the shoes over to the girls, and could contain himself no longer.

"Thank you very much, Ma'am. By the way, I just have to ask and I hope you won't be offended. Are all these children yours?"

I flashed a warm smile his way and replied in a slow, calm tone "Oh, yes, they're all mine. And I have three sons at home." With that I turned and walked out, not looking back. The girls were stifling laughter as we rounded the corner.

"Momma, did you see his face when you told him you had three sons?" Julie was now laughing out loud. "I bet he's still talking about us!"

That was the beginning of many amusing episodes in the life of the Sutcliffe clan. Linnie and I began to buy groceries once every two weeks. He would meet me in town when I got off work, we would do our shopping, and get a sandwich before heading home. He pushed one buggy, I followed with another. We bought vegetables and fruits in gallon cans and usually had at least eight giant boxes of corn flakes. I stood behind Linnie at the checkout counter as he unloaded his cart. This particular day we had a new checker who wasn't familiar with our family. She was almost finished checking the items in Linnie's cart when she smiled, "You must have a big family, Sir."

I smiled innocently, "Oh, that isn't all. This buggy goes with it. We have eight children at home."

Her astonishment was obvious as she floundered through the rest of the order and totaled the bill. As we walked out the store, I could see her whispering to the checker next to her, obviously wondering how on earth we managed with ten people to feed.

Chapter 7

CRISIS OVERCOME

Finally summer gave way to fall and school began. Lin was off to Clemson and the rest of the kids returned to school. Linnie and I had to establish some new rules for the household. When the kids returned home in the afternoon around 3:00 p.m., they were given fifteen minutes to get a snack and get to their bedrooms for study. Thea and Polly were in charge during this time. After study time at 4:30 p.m. their chores began, after which they were free to do whatever they wished until supper.

Being a step-mother is not easy. No one told me it was going to be a cinch. But neither did I spend hours before Linnie and I married musing about the pros and cons of step-parenthood. I just assumed all of the conflicts and problems would somehow "work themselves out." Well, it didn't exactly happen that way.

I knew I must tread softly at first because I didn't want to make any enemies before I could make friends. Working in the kitchen with Polly and Thea, the oldest two girls, I was careful not to intrude on their conversations nor give my opinions unless asked. Before long I found that they would include me in some of their chit-chat about school, boys, and were asking my opinion on different issues. They seemed to accept me as a friend, sometimes a confidant, one who would not run to Daddy with every problem. But Julie was another matter. At 12 years old, Julie had fallen headlong into that difficult time for a girl with the moods and crying spells that go along with it. The more I tried to get close to her, the more she seemed to push me away. I hesitated to take the problem to Linnie because I somehow felt this was one thing that I should try to handle alone.

One night at the supper table, I heard Julie complaining, "I don't have anywhere to put my things. Cindy's clothes take up most of the closet." Julie's face was twisted in a scowl and her long, brown hair hung covering beautiful, blue eyes. Before I could respond, Linnie then looked towards Julie and said, "Young lady, if I have to tell you one more time to keep your hair pinned back when you come to the table, you will get it cut." Linnie's voice was authoritative and I knew he meant every word that he said. He turned to me and said, "Sweetheart, how about checking on this closet business between Cindy and Julie after supper."

After the table had been cleared, and Thea and Polly began washing dishes, I went into Julie's and Cindy's room and divided the closet in half. "Now, Julie, this should be a fair way to keep your things. Cindy, please do not get on Julie's half of the closet. You two girls need to learn how to get along. As you learn to live together in this bedroom, you will be helping our whole family to mold and develop into a real team. And by the way, Julie, please keep your barrettes in or Daddy will make you get your hair cut. You know he means what he says. It is not good to have your hair dragging in your plate. That's why I had Janet's cut last month. She would not keep it pinned back. Please do this for me. Just keep it combed and pinned back, okay?"

"Yes, Ma'am," she replied.

I wanted to be a little more patient with Julie during this difficult period in her development. So, later that night when Linnie and I were talking in our room, I tried to impress on him that he had to be more understanding of Julie during these teenage years rapt with hormonal fluctuations, mood swings, and behavioral shifts. And I knew we would in all probability be facing turbulent waters very soon with Cindy, who was one year younger than Julie.

"I understand what you are saying, Sweetheart. I know it's not easy for a girl to grow up. I've already been through this with Thea and Polly. I understand I must be more understanding! But if I see Julie one more time letting her hair dangle in her eyes and dragging in food at the table, off it comes and that's final!"

I sensed that he had closed the discussion so I decided to drop the subject until a better time.

For several weeks things seemed to be getting a little better between Julie and me. Then one morning after breakfast, Linnie dropped the news before I left for work. "I want you to call someone and make an appointment to get Julie's hair cut. I have warned her, and she apparently does not think I mean what I say. Last night her hair dangled at supper and again this morning. I'm surprised she didn't get syrup from her pancakes caked in her hair."

"Babe, don't be so hasty. Let's talk about it," I pleaded.

"Make the appointment today and get it cut," he demanded, raising his hand signifying that the subject was closed.

I should have asked Linnie to take care of this problem, I thought, for him to make the appointment. I should have explained to him how impossible it was for me, a new mom, to carry Julie to have her hair cut. But I didn't. I should have recognized that a woman's hair is her glory. I didn't think enough of what consequences may occur. The appointment was made and I sent Julie one afternoon after school. The hairdresser was to cut it and give her a soft perm.

When I got home that day I was exhausted from a very busy day at the office and having had to buy groceries after work. It was late; I was hungry and very tired. Polly met me first.

"Mom, Julie's hair is really short. She hasn't come out of her room since she got back from town. I think she's crying. Cindy is with her."

I quickly put down my armload of groceries, forgot my hunger, and went straight to Julie's room. I was expecting the worst, and when I opened the door I was very surprised. Her hair *was* cut shorter than I expected but looked very nice, not too curly. "Oh, Julie, it looks beautiful!" I reassured her.

She was staring at the mirror and glared through her tears at me. Her face was red, and swollen from crying. "I hate it. It looks awful. I will <u>never</u> go back to school and face my friends!" Her entire body was limp, and she turned her face away.

I knew my reassurance was not what she needed, so I left her alone for a while. Coming back through the kitchen, I asked the girls if they would finish the meal for me because I didn't want any supper. How could I eat with this on my mind? Julie came through behind me with her bathrobe and towel and disappeared in the bathroom. Her shoulders sagged beneath the weight of her unhappiness, and I wondered how on earth I could help her now.

"Oh, Father", I prayed desperately. "I need your help here. With the growing pressures at work coupled with all these pressures at home, I don't know where to turn, what to do next. I need your intercession and your wisdom." My thoughts were interrupted by the telephone.

"Mom, it's for you", Thea said. It's Julie's teacher.

"That's all I need", I thought. "What could be wrong now?" I took the receiver and tried vainly to appear calm but could feel myself getting extremely tense and nervous.

"I hated to make this call", she said, "because I am aware of your family's circumstances, but I am concerned about Julie. She is not herself at school and seems to be distracted in class lately. She is failing spelling every week, and anyone can learn to spell."

"I am aware of some of Julie's trouble," I replied. She is going through a difficult period of adjustment. I assure you I will have a talk with her and do what I can at home to help her catch up her studies. I'm sure she will begin to improve with some help from home."

As I was expressing my appreciation for her concern, Julie appeared from the bathroom and walked toward her bedroom. I became suddenly numb. She had wet her hair. It was drenched and she hadn't even bothered to towel dry it. Her bangs hung loosely covering her eyes, and water dripped on the floor with each step. Julie strode past, leering at me with one eye covered by unruly strands of hair. I managed to end the phone conversation and hung up the receiver. Something within me snapped. I stood in the kitchen, experiencing half anger and half desperation. "Is she trying to punish me?" An overwhelming wave of despair washed over me. I fought the tears back and hurried to her room. She was standing in front of the mirror, hair dripping wet, water all over the carpet and the dresser.

"Julie!" I screamed, for the first time giving expression to my anger and frustration. I walked up beside her and caught her by the arm, by this time crying myself.

"What are you trying to do to me? I love you, I love all of you, but I can't stand this anymore." The more I said, the harder I cried. "I have tried to be good to you, I've tried to do what Daddy tells me also. What are you doing this for? Why? Why?" I started to cry uncontrollably, and my body was shaking all over.

I don't remember much of what happened after that. I heard Polly scream, "Eddie! Go get Grandma Sutcliffe, quick!" Cindy was screaming. Thea stood there, wild eyed. Julie was crying.

I must have cried for what seemed like hours. The next thing I remember, Linnie's mom was there. I was in my bed, and Cindy was bathing my face with a cold washcloth. I felt numb, and totally consumed with despair. I couldn't stop crying. "Don't tell Linnie, Grandma. She stood at my bedside, a tower of strength and grit. Please don't tell him; he'll be so mad at Julie. Please."

"We've already called Linnie," Grandma stated, matter-of-factly. "He needs to be here. He's already on his way home from work. Everything's gonna be alright."

I then heard Linnie's voice in the kitchen. "Where is Julie?" he demanded. I knew Linnie would address the problem swiftly and with fierce determination. His voice penetrated my sorrow, and my mind focused once again.

"Linnie, Linnie, come here", I called desperately to him. He came and leaned over the bed, and I held him close for a long time, still sobbing. "Please don't be angry at Julie. She didn't mean to upset me, and I'm partly to blame. Please try to understand her."

"Are you all right?" he asked, cupping my face in his hands. "You know you are the most important person in the world to me, don't you? You know that I love you, don't you?"

"Yes, just please don't get angry at Julie." He didn't make any promises, but arose and left the bedroom. Several minutes later he was back. "Julie is outside the door. She wants to see you," he said. She says she just wants to apologize."

Julie came into the dark bedroom slowly, her body shaking from the sobs. She dropped to her knees beside the bed and caught my hand. "Oh, Mom, Mom, I'm so sorry. Honest I am. I love you. Please don't cry anymore. I'll dry my hair. I'll keep it out of my eyes, too. And Polly and Thea said they can help me fix it for tomorrow. If you'll forgive me, I'll never be any more trouble, ever again."

"Oh, Julie, I'm sorry, too. Please forgive me for losing my temper at you. We've got to pull together, you and me. Don't you see? I love you. We'll fix your hair and it won't be long before it's grown out again." Now, go and let them fix it for you. Remember, I love you very much."

Linnie came back by the bedside as she left the room. "I have told Julie she can stay home from school tomorrow and minister to you. I believe she realizes where she was wrong, and who knows, maybe you two will be closer because of this night."

I cannot say that Julie never gave us anymore trouble after that crisis. Well, we dealt with heartache in one way or another with every one of our children. And I never really knew what Linnie said to Julie when he came home that night. Our relationship did take a turning point after I went to pieces. We learned together to love, forgive, and hold each other through every single situation.

Julie fell head over heels in love with a boy named Terry in our church when she was fourteen, and he was all she wanted to talk about. We never let the kids date until they were sixteen, but she asked anyway. So, Terry came over and visited with her in our living room for two hours every week. And they sat together at church every Sunday. She was allowed to talk to him on the phone once a week for ten minutes. This went on until Julie was sixteen, when she was urged to get a job.

All of the kids began working at sixteen and she was no exception. I went to Julie on several occasions and told her to go put in applications at several job sites around the area. She was driving and could drive herself back and forth to work in our extra car. Well, Julie did get a job, and worked at a local florist until she graduated from high school. Realizing Julie had a talent and passion for flowers and making arrangements, Mrs. Emma Lou Fort took Julie as her protégé. Julie truly enjoyed working at the florist and actually looked forward to her time there learning about floral design.

Julie came to us at the end of her junior year and asked if she could go to summer school to graduate a year early. After graduation from summer school, she wanted to get married.

"You let Eddie graduate a year early and I want the same privilege. Terry and I want to get married in July after summer school. I know you can't afford to give me a big wedding, but we can have something small. It's okay."

Linnie and I discussed Julie's proposal for a long time. And we finally determined that Julie had matured into a young lady ready to leave home, eager for independence, and prepared to embrace marriage. She was happy, made us laugh, and was a joy to be around. It was clear to everyone that Julie was truly in love. So, we called Julie back into our bedroom, and gave our permission. "Mom and I talked about this, and we've decided to let you go to summer school, and get married like you've asked," Dad said. Julie was ecstatic! She jumped up and hugged both of us, her eyes dancing with delight. "Thank you, Dad! Oh, Mom thank you! I'm so happy!"

We planned an intimate wedding ceremony at our church. I

made the bridesmaid dresses for her sisters. We made phone calls to order flowers, and Julie helped to arrange most of the flowers for her wedding. Cindy and Polly provided the music, and we enjoyed fellowship afterwards with family and friends at our church fellowship hall. Julie walked down the aisle that day, truly a woman who had come of age. Truly a beautiful, blissful bride.

Well, life has its twists and turns. And some bends in Julie's life journey were hard as nails. After ten years of marriage, Julie's husband, abruptly one day, said that he wanted a divorce. Throughout this heartbreaking time in Julie's life, I witnessed her emerge as a strong, resolute woman. And a wife who persevered with integrity in the midst of hurt and shattered dreams. After Julie's divorce, she went back to school, studied with dedication, and graduated as a Licensed Practical Nurse. She moved to Columbia, bought a place of her own, made enormous improvements on her home, (and did much of the work herself), and began a career in healthcare. Over time, Julie met and fell in love with a wonderful man, Jay Reynolds, whom she is married to today. They make us laugh, feel loved, and so appreciated. We are so happy for them!

Today, Julie is the most selfless, loving, and gracious human being that I know. She loves with a heart as deep as the ocean and wide as the east is from the west. And what a worker! Ask our son-in-law, Dr. Rodney Fitzgibbon, who his most valued employee is, and he's sure to say without hesitation, Julie Reynolds. No project is too daunting for Julie. She has independently remodeled bathrooms, can wire, hang and prepare sheetrock, paint like a pro, landscape a yard in "two shakes", and has assisted in home improvement projects in numerous of the family's homes. She is our "take charge" one, and is extremely attentive to Linnie and me, and our entire family. And we know if Julie ever finds out we're under the weather, we're sure to get a phone call, and several visits to either clean, cook, or work in the garden. She loves and nurtures all of us, and keeps in touch with us weekly.

"Oh God, you do have plans for us," I thought, smiling in my heart! "And you walk with me through many turbulent times of crisis. Thank you for helping us overcome. Thank you, God, for being there every step of the way. And thank you for giving us Julie, who is a precious joy to my soul."

Chapter 8

A TURNING POINT

"**M**om, we're leaving!"

Thea's voice reached me and I heard the back door closing behind her. The familiar sound of the car motor told me I was alone in the house. Even though the day had just begun, I felt totally spent, drained of all energy, unable to cope with another day. "Thank goodness I have the day off", I thought to myself. "I couldn't face the pressure at work today, not today." My hands were trembling slightly as I poured a cup of coffee and sank wearily into a chair, feeling an overwhelming sense of despair. Outside, the sun was already bathing everything in its golden beauty. The trees in the woods glistened in the sun as the wind moved them to and fro. The sunlight streamed in the kitchen window and seemed to lay its radiance on our kitchen table, trying to remind me of God's wondrous beauty of His world. I wasn't feeling very thankful and, as I toyed with my coffee the memory of that morning returned. It had begun as a normal day, as normal as it could be trying to get nine people up, fed, and off to work and school. Linnie had left for work long before the bombshell dropped, and I was glad he was spared the confrontation with Eddie that morning.

Thea and Polly had come to me again about Eddie's attitude.

"Eddie won't do his chores", Thea complained, a note of sharpness in her voice. "He won't listen to anybody anymore. We can't even study in the afternoon because he plays his stereo so loud."

"Thea, it isn't quite that bad", Polly's soft voice interrupted. Polly, the compassionate, understanding one, always trying to soften even the worst situation, turned to me, and I could sense that she was deeply troubled.

"Mom, we've tried. We really have. But Thea is right. I don't know what's come over Eddie lately. I hate to complain so much, knowing how much you have to worry about as it is. But something has to be done. We just can't seem to get along with him at all."

Wearily I assured them I would have a talk with Eddie and try to get to the bottom of his problem. This wasn't the first time the kids had complained about Eddie's behavior. His almost hostile attitude was a complete enigma to me. I had talked with him a great deal about getting married again after I met Linnie, and he was all for it. When we told the children we had decided to put the families together, Eddie seemed as thrilled as the rest. Out of all eight kids, I thought Eddie would adjust more quickly because of his maturity and understanding. Now I had to face the fact that he was the only one who wasn't adjusting.

I knocked hesitantly on his bedroom door.

"Come in."

He looked up as I entered and I couldn't help but notice how much he resembled his father. The same curly blond hair that sometimes fell on his forehead in an almost perfect wave, the same eyes that seemed to sparkle every time he laughed. It had been ages since I had heard that happy laugh.

"Eddie, I want to talk for a few minutes." I dreaded this talk, just as I had dreaded all the others we'd had lately. Every time we talked, we seemed to end up arguing and getting nowhere.

"Eddie, why can't you get along with the other kids? What seems to be the problem?"

"I get along."

"But, there's something wrong. You were so happy when I

decided to re-marry. You seemed to be thrilled to know you would have so many brothers and sisters. Now, it's almost as if you hate it here or . . ."

"I'm fine!" he almost shouted at me, throwing his books together and turning away from me. "I just wish everybody would get off my back."

"Nobody's on your back, Eddie, at least we don't mean to be. I just wish you'd level with me about why your attitude has changed so much. I desperately want this marriage to work and am happier than I've ever been. I'm sure this is what God wants for all of us. But when a problem comes up, we can't bury our heads in the sand. I want to help, son." My voice trembled with emotion as the tears welled in my eyes, and I tried to blink them away.

"Mom, really, it's nothing, believe me. His voice softened as he turned to face me. "Look, I don't mean to be ugly. It's just that sometimes I get tired of people telling me what to do . . . when to study, when to do my chores, even when I can take a bath. I feel like I'm in the army. I feel caged, pinned in."

"But, Eddie, we have to have rules. You're old enough to know that. We agreed on the rules, everyone did. We explained to all of you that the only way to operate the house with ten people was to operate as a team, with everyone doing his share. You have to pull your share of the load, just like everybody else."

"I know. I'll try to do better, Mom, honest. Just give me time."

I could sense he had closed the subject and was relieved to let him gather his books and leave.

"At least he knows I want to understand", I told myself, trying to somehow ease the pain I felt for not being able to solve this problem.

"Help me with this, Lord", I prayed. "I feel so helpless and overwhelmed right now. I need Your wisdom and understanding."

The sun's rays were quickly warming the kitchen but I felt a sudden chill. As happens when the emotional thermometer is reading "Low", doubts and questions began to creep in. Why Eddie? Why did it have to be Eddie causing friction? All the other children had adjusted beautifully to a new life, new parents, new rules . . . except Eddie. Even Julie was trying to do her share. For weeks I had watched the situation grow from bad to worse, watched as he changed from a happy, carefree, mature fifteen-year-old to a sullen, obnoxious boy. His face mirrored unhappiness, and with each talk we had I felt even more confused, more helpless. He was so happy with my decision to marry again.

Even after the trauma of moving to a strange new home and new school, he had appeared content and happy. All the kids got along well together, almost as if they had always been together, always one family. Everything worked so perfectly, and now this. Maybe all my friends were right. Maybe putting two families together was an impossible dream. Everybody said we'd never be able to do it. They said we were crazy for even thinking it would work.

"Oh, God, what am I going to do?" The flood of tears I had held back all morning broke through and fell on my tightly clasped hands. "Please help me to help Eddie. Please give me strength where there is none. Keep the doubts away and give me an answer to this dilemma."

After my first husband, Ed passed away, Eddie tackled jobs around the house that a man would do. When we went camping for a weekend, Eddie would take charge and completely assemble our tent and get all the equipment set up. If an appliance broke around the house, I called Eddie to repair it. One day my waffle iron stopped working and I asked him to take a look at it. Eddie took it apart, rewired it, and we were back to cooking waffles in no time. We had a small camping trailer that Eddie's dad had built several months before his death in which we carried our camping equipment. Eddie asked me one day if he could put lights on it. Since his dad had taught him a great deal about electricity and wiring, I gave him my approval. Eddie completely wired the trailer, installing switches on the outside. After this accomplishment, Eddie put up outside lights on our home so we could light the backyard. If a bike was broken, Cindy and Mark would immediately call for Eddie. He was the general "fix-it" man around the house.I began to lean on him heavily without realizing it, and he accepted the responsibility with maturity which only God could have provided. If I was sick, he would get the other kids fed and see that they were ready for bed at night. He began to get up early every morning, shower, and cook breakfast. His favorite was "orange pancakes", and the kids still tease him about putting orange juice in his pancakes! He says they are good! Cindy and Mark were placed in his care if I ever had to be away, and they knew that when Eddie spoke, they listened. I even asked his opinions when making decisions around the house. He had really been a man during those years. Why was he now acting so childish?

Suddenly, like a light flooding a dark room, the truth struck me - - Eddie had become a man - - without having the privilege of being a boy! From a child of eleven to a man of twelve - - forced by God's timing to accept adulthood. For four years he had acted and reacted as an adult, accepting the responsibilities of an adult, doing the chores of an adult - - and now we were expecting him to be a boy again in a family with older sisters and brothers, and it was proving hard, almost impossible, for him to handle. All this time I felt he would be relieved to be free of heavy responsibilities, to be able to enjoy being a typical teen-ager, having a father who could take over and handle everything. How could I have been so blind! His place of authority, of honor, had been snatched from him. He had been replaced by someone he hardly knew who made all decisions and to whom I went for advice, a father who was now filling the role he had filled for four years.

"I've really muddled this up good", I thought to myself, wiping the tears away. I felt a pang of guilt mingled with an overwhelming sense of relief that through the maze of questions and searching there may be a glimmer of light. "How can I possibly correct the damage that has been done and help Eddie cope with this?"

"Oh, God, please forgive me," I cried out. "Please give me your peace and show me the way. Make your presence known to me so I will have the courage and strength to work this out."

Emotionally drained, I got up and poured the untouched cup of coffee down the drain. I had to shake this feeling of fear, thinking that things may not work out. As I lingered at the sink, wondering what to do, my eyes wandered out the kitchen window over the freshly plowed field behind the house and the woods beyond. The beautiful golden and crimson leaves glistened like a splash of water colors. The wind was blowing, turning the leaves from one hue to another. I watched for a long while, almost paralyzed by the beauty. I'd never noticed them being so radiant before.

"This is truly a "touch of the Master's hand", I thought. "Thank you God." I could slowly feel the peace for which I had asked settling over me. Without hearing God's voice, I definitely heard his message. And what had been an almost insurmountable problem two hours before didn't seem so gigantic now as I felt the assurance of God's presence and His direction. I paused for just a moment longer. "Thank you, Lord, for reminding me that I can't manage anything alone. Thanks for showing me you are in control. This is probably the first of many crises for us as a family, so You'll just have to take over and make this marriage work."

With a new burst of joy I brushed away the last trace of tears and began to hum softly as I turned to face the mountain of clothes to be laundered.

Eddie's problem didn't disappear miraculously simply because I had discovered the cause of it. Linnie and I both realized that it was going to take time and patience to work it out. Lin had left for college recently, and we knew that Thea, next in age, had looked forward to the time when she would be the oldest, a position that in our family carried certain privileges as well as responsibilities. We couldn't expect her to give up that place because of Eddie's quandary.

I prayed about the matter daily, and my heart went out to Eddie when I saw him so unhappy. Linnie and I called the kids together on numerous occasions for a family conference, stressing the importance of pulling together. Both of us expressed our confidence in our marriage and in the children, assuring them of our love and concern for all of them. We tried to air their gripes openly and attempted to iron out the big differences. I had more talks with Eddie, but now that I understood his problem, the talks seemed to be easier for both of us. I constantly assured him of my understanding and love and asked him to do his part to make the family succeed.

I called Thea and Polly together one night and attempted to explain what Eddie was going through, and I asked for their understanding and cooperation. I assured them of my confidence that this crisis would pass, and we would all look back and smile, wondering why we were ever so concerned.

"But he bugs me sometimes when he is so surly", one of them said.

"I'm sure he does. But remember we all have ways that "bug" each other. We all have peculiarities that other people have to accept. Just living together, all ten of us, with all of our differences heaped together, is not going to be easy. Just try to give Eddie a little extra understanding right now because of his struggle. Your dad and I have talked and prayed about this situation, and we have some ideas of how to address the problem."

We decided to allow Eddie, who already had his driver's license, to drive to school and Thea could drive home. We asked the older girls to try to avoid giving Eddie any direct instructions regarding chores. Linnie or I would ask him to do whatever needed to be done. At the same time I enlisted Mark's help and asked him to call on Eddie for any task that he may need assistance on, whether it be fixing a bike tire or helping him assemble a model car, which Mark was collecting. I began to make a special effort to lean on Eddie for small tasks which he could do. I called him into the kitchen one afternoon after school.

"Eddie, I really need an electrical cord run underground

from the house to the shed outside where the extra freezer and refrigerator are. Daddy is so busy right now, he can't get to it. Think you can handle it?"

I caught a slight sparkle in his eyes as he replied, "I think so, Mom."

"O.K. I'm putting you in charge of that project. You'll have to measure the distance, pick up the materials at the hardware store in town, and do the job. Daddy will check it when you are through.

Eddie not only ran the line, but he installed switches, an accomplishment I'm sure made him feel two years older. Linnie had someone check the work, and he said Eddie had done a super job. Anytime one of my electrical appliances failed to work, I called Eddie and asked him to take a look.

Another day Linnie was trying to finish the electrical work in the den which had been added on the house when we got married. He was struggling with two switches that wouldn't work right.

"How about asking Eddie to give me a hand," he called, a note of impatience evident in his voice. Eddie pitched in and after working alongside Linnie for a few minutes, discovered that a wire had been connected wrong. Even though being outdone by his sixteen-year-old son put a slight dent in Linnie's ego, it was worth it. And it sure gave Eddie a tremendous "boost".

This new approach had dual success. It helped Eddie's problem in immeasurable proportions while taking a great deal of responsibility from Linnie's shoulders. After several months, I began to detect a gradual change in Eddie's disposition, especially around the other kids. He began to join the family in the den instead of closing himself in his room. I also noted a change in Polly's and Thea's attitude. From a period of not speaking unless passing a caustic remark, the three of them began to talk of school, teachers, and other things of interest to teenagers. Eddie built and installed two stereo speakers in our den, ran the wire, and did a professional job. Anytime there was electrical work to be done, Linnie would say, "Call Eddie. Eddie's the electrical expert around the Sutcliffe house."

One day after that Eddie approached me and asked if he could talk to Linnie and me. "I'd like to finish school a year early", he said. I want to attend Clemson in the fall of next year. I will have enough credits to do it and some to spare. I've been working really hard these last three years and can get scholarships and grants to help me go without a lot of debt." The three of us discussed the matter and we gave him our permission to do so. Eddie went on to college the next year, made the Dean's List, and graduated with honors and a master's degree. Another boost to his ego.

The marvelous miracle of the crisis was that the children all emerged from it stronger, more capable of dealing with other people, and more aware of their own shortcomings. They are as close today as any brothers and sisters could possibly be. As I predicted, they can all remember the "rough times" now and laugh at them.

Isn't it a miracle how God can take any situation, no matter how seemingly complex, and in time unravel a beautiful outcome?

"All things work together for good to those that love God." I truly believe it!

Chapter 9

IT'S A MOUSE!

You might say that life in the Sutcliffe household became routine, but you certainly couldn't say it was ever dull! As we settled into a schedule, the chaotic, hectic conditions of the first weeks together faded. However, each week brought a new challenge, a different crisis, or at times, a touch of humor to maybe lift a cloud of doubt. It always seemed that whenever I became discouraged under the load of caring for such a large family, something would happen in our lives to brighten the day and give me a fresh "boost." I can only acknowledge that "God truly does work in mysterious ways" because only He knew how discouraged I became at times during the first months of adjusting.

Just when everything seemed to be going smoothly and I felt as if we'd make it, we discovered another problem. We had mice in our house!

Now, I will tackle roaches, spiders, ants, really all kinds of bugs. But, I am deathly afraid of a mouse! If anything will send me screaming to perch on top of the table or chair, it's a mouse, whether he's 3 or 10 inches long. We discovered that in re-wiring the house for the addition, the electrical workers left a small hole in the utility room floor, through which the new inhabitants were gaining entrance to warmer lodgings. Linnie and I were sitting at the breakfast table one morning after the kids had cleared out of the kitchen. All of a sudden Linnie said quickly, "Look out, there's a mouse!"

"A mouse! Where?" I screamed as I jumped up in a chair.

"He went in the living room", Linnie replied and ran to get a fly swatter. By this time all of the kids were gathering in the kitchen.

"What happened?" one of them asked.

"It's a mouse!"

"Look at Momma," Janet laughed excitedly. "Daddy has him cornered in the living room!"

"Let me see!" Mark had just arrived, not wanting to be left out of the hunt.

Linnie handed me another swatter. "I'll see if I can corner the mouse in the living room. You stand at the door and don't let him out under the door."

Not wanting to admit my utter terror in front of the kids and realizing that Linnie's patience with me was quickly waning, I bravely stepped down from the chair and took up vigil to guard the door as Linnie closed it behind him. I could hear him chasing the unwanted guest, slapping here and there with the swatter, and as I leaned over toward the crack under the door, the frightened mouse darted under the door, between my legs, and down the hall into my bedroom. I screamed and the kids laughed more than ever.

"There he goes, Momma," Mark jumped up and down, clapping his hands in delight as the other kids watched cowardice creeping across my face. Linnie came out of the living room manned with his "weapon".

"Daddy, he went in your bedroom," Janet shouted!

"That's all right. We'll get him with a trap later," Dad replied.

"Oh, no!" I was already shaking my head, panicking. "I'll not sleep in the room tonight if that rat is in there."

"It's not a wharf rat, sweetheart. It's only a tiny mouse who is a lot more scared of you than you are of him." Linnie was beginning to enjoy my fear along with the kids.

"It might be a mouse to you," I said, "but he's a rat to me, and I want him out of my bedroom now."

Fifteen minutes later, after closing Linnie up in the bathroom with the varmint, chasing him all over our bedroom (Linnie did the chasing, I did the overseeing from on top of our bed), Linnie finally "did him in" and ended the mêlée. Picking up the limp mouse, Linnie was still panting from the chase. I said, "Golly, Babe, he looks so helpless. Maybe we shouldn't have killed him."

The kids burst out laughing.

He looked at me with a mixture of consternation and bewilderment, threw up his hands and walked out toward the back door.

"Women!" he muttered as he opened the door. "Women!"

Chapter 10

THAT'S NOT FAIR!

When I accepted the challenge of being mother to eight children instead of three, I knew that I must "tread softly" from the first day regarding the treatment of all the children as mine. It was imperative that I be fair and equal in my dealings with all of them. A friend of mine had remarried after divorce, bringing together six children. She began to resent her new husband correcting her children and sometimes felt he was favoring his own. Their marriage lasted less than a year.

It is difficult to be fair to our children all of the time because we are human and make mistakes. But the job is twice as challenging when there are two families involved. Linnie and I had an understanding at the outset of our marriage to deal with treating all of the children as _ours_ - not mine and his – but _ours._ It became a source of irritation to me on occasions when introduced to people and they would ask, "Now, which are yours and which are his?" I learned to quietly smile calmly and say "Why they are all ours!" That took any embarrassment away from the kids, and at the same time gave them a sense of pride in being considered one, big family instead of two separate ones.

I realized that I must treat all of the kids as mine or trouble would be around the corner. If I let Janet or Julie overstep set limits without punishment, Mark or Cindy would be quick to notice and also quick to resent it. I also knew that Linnie must have the same attitude so we could all pull together. We had talked about this before we got married, and I count it as another of God's miracles the way both of us responded to this difficult task. As the days moved into weeks, my hesitancy to correct some of the kids faded as we began to operate as one family, brought together by God.

If I gave Janet a special privilege, I was careful to allow the same privilege for Mark. If Polly was permitted to stay out late on a particular request, I would try to remember that when Eddie made a similar request. Several months before Julie was sixteen, she came to me with a request that she be granted permission to attend a friend's birthday party with an escort. She had not forgotten that several years before, Polly had received permission to attend an event with an escort before she was sixteen. I took Julie's request to Linnie, and we agreed that she should be allowed to go.

So many times in a home you can hear a familiar cry from a disgruntled youngster, "that isn't fair!" We have heard these words in our home, but they have been exclaimed only a few times. In most cases our young people have felt that we were trying our best as parents to be fair and equal in all matters.

In the matter of responsibilities, we assigned chores so as to be fair to all and not load one or two with more responsibility than the rest. Naturally, the four older ones assumed more responsibility than the four younger. We were careful to assign duties equally to Mark and Janet, also Julie and Cindy. Jealously was one problem we didn't need and it was one we never had.

I have seen many homes in which partiality was shown between children and it is truly a tragedy. It is sad that parents cannot recognize this situation in the home before it affects the children involved. I know of a couple who favor one child, requiring a minimum of responsibility from her, while the younger sister gets saddled with all the chores such as washing, cooking, cleaning, and on occasion, mowing the yard. The heavily laden sister is growing into adulthood with a feeling of resentment toward her parents and toward her sister. At the same time, the carefree, pampered sister is growing up but not necessarily into mature adulthood. She has never known set rules, comes and goes when she pleases, and is beginning to think the world and its pleasures were created for her. Thus, two lives have been affected by this unfairness.

I have always been concerned about the problem of partiality in some homes and immediately faced the possibility of it becoming a problem in a mixed family relationship. It is not easy to discipline someone else's child. I knew the temptation would arise to let Linnie's children by with less severe discipline than my own. The temptation for him would be the same. So, we met the matter head-on, discussed it openly, as we did everything, and decided on a course of action. We agreed it would not be an easy task, but all eight children must be dealt with as one family, getting equal and fair treatment in matters of discipline, chores, privileges, etc.

One weekend Polly was home from college and asked if she, Julie and Cindy could go to play tennis on Saturday night for several hours. After they left, Janet came in and said, "I don't think it was quite fair, them going off and not even inviting Mark and me." She was hurt and didn't understand, but I reminded her of occasions two years before when Lin, Thea, Eddie and Polly would go bowling or to a movie and Julie, Cindy, Mark and she would not be invited. I said, "Janet, remember the older you get, the more freedom you will have and the more privileges you will enjoy. If you got to do anything you wanted and go anywhere you wanted at twelve years of age, what would you do when you became sixteen?" I'm not really sure if she ever really understood what I was saying, but I am sure I gave her food for thought.

As the children grew, matured and their responsibilities grew, I tried daily to keep this philosophy of equality. I was tempted many times to call Cindy to do special kitchen work, realizing that she showed a great interest in cooking, but I also realized it wasn't fair to her or Julie so I tried to alternate when an extra kitchen detail was needed. I admit that it wasn't the "easy way" because Julie expressed a limited interest in the kitchen, but she always pitched in anytime I needed her and did a great job.

As Mark began to help his dad with the farming chores outside, I began to give Janet more inside chores to equal the load and also begin her training in the kitchen. She moved into the kitchen very reluctantly and the first week or two, she had to be called from her playing to remind her it was time to clean up the dishes after mealtime. The girls always took turns washing, rinsing, and drying. After Janet was required to dry and put away the dishes every time she was late in the kitchen, she decided she'd better take the responsibility of being on time. I never believed in coaxing children to do a task, and I tried to find other ways to teach them to accept certain responsibilities without having to remind them over and over again.

Unbelievable as it may seem, where the eight of them sat in the car became an immediate concern. So we decided the fair way was to go by age. The oldest sat in the front of our station wagon, the next three in the back seat, and the youngest two had to sit behind the back seat. Youngsters in a small family would never identify with this, but it was a "giant step" up for our kids to graduate from the very back of the wagon to the back seat as the older ones left for college. They felt very big indeed when this happened.

After several weeks in our new home, another problem arose - trying to prepare foods that everyone liked. The two families had different eating habits and did not like the same foods. Trying to please ten people was impossible, I knew from the beginning. Janet liked cereal for breakfast and would eat nothing else, Eddie disliked cereal. My children loved potato salad, Linnie's did not. His kids liked bacon with their grits, mine liked hash. This called for another "meeting of the minds", and Linnie and I decided on a solution. I would try to please at least some of them with each meal, planning my menus so that during a given week I would have included the preferences of each family member. This would call for adjustment on the part of all of us, including Linnie and me.

The kids were told of our decision and that they would be expected to eat a small portion of whatever was set before them. It was a real struggle the first year, watching Janet move her eggs around her plate at breakfast, hoping that in so doing they would somehow disappear before her eyes. For six months when we had pancakes for breakfast she would cut all the outside from the pancake, leaving about three or four small pieces which she ate very slowly and laboriously. The first time I served asparagus casserole, I saw about five or six faces which mirrored abhorrence. They each took a "very" slim spoonful and ate it reluctantly. After serving it about four or five times, I had to double the recipe because they were arguing over who would get the last helping! When we served greens, it was a special accomplishment for them. I've seen Janet drink two glasses of tea trying to get one helping of greens down. And Eddie would cover his turnips with a heavy layer of sugar to be able to eat them.

In this way, we were being fair to all of the members of the family and at the same time teaching them to acquire a taste for all kinds of foods. I certainly couldn't fix a separate meal for each person in a family of ten and I had never done it before.

A friend told me one time that she lets her family get their own breakfast because each of the children likes a different menu. So she stays out of the kitchen, there is no family breakfast, and it's "everyone for himself." In our home, Linnie and I chose to get up early at five o'clock, in order to prepare breakfast for our children. Sometimes it was a hot meal, other mornings cereal was served. We believed that starting the day off with breakfast together was extremely important and contributed to our family being cohesive, strong, and united. So often today, parents do not prepare breakfast allowing the children to fend for themselves. Consequently, many children leave for school without eating. It was our belief that rising early enough to serve a family meal was well worth the effort.

The necessity of eating a little of everything at mealtime didn't go over too well at first, but it wasn't long before I noticed the kids eating strange looking recipes without complaining. Most of them today can eat almost anything. And I wondered for a while if Janet would ever be able to do the impossible – clean a plate full of grits, bacon, and eggs!

Daddy had his share of "forced eating", too. He found a new recipe one day for "southern cornbread" and asked me to try it, which I did. Well, he raved after eating it that it was the "only real cornbread" he had eaten in a long time. Needless to say, no one else around the table shared his enthusiasm for this newly discovered "delicacy" in the menu, but we each ate a little anyway. After preparing his cornbread several times, the girls and I agreed to cook some of our cornbread which he had to eat. What's fair for one was fair for all!

One Saturday during a very cold winter when our gas supply had been rationed, Linnie announced that we would have to cut and haul wood for the fireplace. He told me to stay at the house and the kids could load the wood onto the truck as he cut it. I didn't feel it was fair to require the children to work while I sat at home. Polly had a friend visiting for the weekend so they stayed at home and prepared my Sunday dinner while the rest of the family went to the woods. It was a family adventure with everyone pitching in doing his share as we formed a line, passing the cut wood from one to another and loading it on the truck. I paid for it the next day with very sore muscles, but it was a joyful experience, sharing the work together.

The first Sunday in our new home was chaotic, to say the least. We hadn't organized our family yet and no one had a specific job to do. I got up at 8:00 a.m., thinking two hours should be plenty of time to be ready for church. Well, after cooking two cups of grits, one pound of bacon and one dozen eggs, getting everyone up, eating, getting the dishes done, and preparing lunch ahead of time, I was a little less than "rested and renewed" for Sunday worship. And we were late for church! To top it off, while walking up the church steps behind Janet, I glanced down at her shoes and realized that, in our rush to get to church, she had forgotten to change her shoes. To my dismay, Janet was wearing torn, dirty keds with her Sunday dress! Thereby came my first resolution – to get better organized!

And there was the day I left a note for the girls to fry pork chops for supper. Well, they did – thirty-two pork chops, to be exact! We enjoyed pork chops that night, but the girls learned a lesson in how much to prepare for ten people. (And I learned a lesson, too - not to expect my girls to know certain things without being told.)

Lessons like these were plentiful during the first months in our home with ten family members sharing their space. We have come a long way since then, many times reflecting on memories like these I have shared with you. But our children have come a long way and have developed into well-adjusted adults who are contributing to our society in a positive way. We are immensely proud of all of them.

Chapter 11

OUR FIRST CHRISTMAS

The weeks turned into months and before I realized what had happened, it was Christmas - - our first Christmas together! As I frantically searched for gifts for everybody, I wondered how the holidays would be. It surely couldn't be as lonely for me as it was the past four years. Lin would be coming home soon from college, and the kids would be out of school for two weeks. They had all given me their Christmas lists, and I found it exciting shopping for each one.

Lin arrived home on Friday and we got ready to trim the tree. Linnie relaxed in his favorite chair after supper dishes were done, and Julie and Cindy began pulling the lights from the boxes that had been packed away in the attic.

"You need some lights on this side, Julie", Linnie said. Julie moved toward the back of the tree with a string of brightly colored lights.

"Back here, on this side", Linnie motioned.

"Janet, you and Mark work close to the bottom of the tree with the ornaments and let the taller kids work on the top", I said.

Janet, her brown eyes dancing with excitement, stood impatiently holding an ornament, anxious to be first to place one on the tree. Mark could hardly contain himself and was trying to hold up a string of lights for Thea.

"Mark, you and Janet come back here and wait until the lights are on the tree. Then both of you can help decorate". I reached out and caught Mark's arm, gently pulling him back from the tree.

Lin came in the den carrying two sandwiches and a glass of tea. "Boy, that's going to be a beautiful tree! Momma, I raided the refrigerator. Hope you don't mind. After eating the food at college, I can't seem to get enough of home cooking. If you're thinking of getting rid of those biscuits from supper, don't. I'll get rid of them for you later tonight." He flashed me a smile and sank into a chair to devour his sandwiches. "I'll just sit here and oversee this project. If you guys need an expert opinion, here I am."

"Brother, dear, if you're going to criticize, you can get up and help", Polly teased.

"By the way, where's your other brother. He's not too good to help decorate this tree. Hey, Eddie, get your lazy self out here and help this work crew."

I held my breath, not knowing what reaction we were going to get. Glancing over at Linnie, I was reassured by a quick wink and a loving smile which told me not to worry.

Moments later Eddie poked his head out of his bedroom door. "What's the matter?" he said. "You amateurs can't decorate a tree without the expert help of pros? Come on, Lin, let's show these helpless females how it should be done!"

Lin gulped down the last of his tea, jumped up and took the remainder of the lights from Julie and Cindy and, with Eddie's help, strung them around the tree. When they finished, they stepped back, and shook hands in agreement that the job was well done.

"Now, ladies, that the hard part is over, you can finish putting the trinkets on the tree", Lin grinned. "Hey, Mark you and Janet come on over here, too." Janet and Mark then hung an array of decorations all around the lower portion to finish up our first Christmas tree as a family.

As Lin and Eddie sat on the floor to watch, I sighed with relief. Eddie was laughing, taking part again, and I was thanking God silently for that laughter and for the change in his behavior and disposition. And the younger two were included much to their delight. Linnie sensed my relief and gratitude and came over and sat by me on the sofa. Putting his arm around me, he pulled me close and kissed me on the cheek.

"Ah, ha!" Polly exclaimed, spotting us. "Smooching in public!" Everybody looked at us and laughed, and Linnie kissed me again. "Just thought since you were all looking, I'd give you something to see," he said, and we all laughed together.

When the last icicle had been carefully placed, we all sat there, drinking in the beauty of the tree and the joy of the season.

"I guess you kids know God has really blessed us and been good to us," I said, as Janet snuggled up to me on one side, squirming as Linnie reached down and tugged at her hair. "We all have our health, a beautiful home, and we have each other. I think this Christmas is going to be the best ever! And we need to always remember whose birthday we celebrate tomorrow – Jesus Christ! He is always the "reason for the season". And now, I think we'd better think about turning in. Tomorrow is Christmas, and I still have a few presents to wrap."

I kissed Janet and Mark goodnight and reminded them to brush their teeth. After everyone had left the den, Linnie and I sat together for a few more moments, watching the lights on the tree reflecting magical colors in the window.

"Quarter." It was his favorite expression for wanting to know what I was thinking.

"Oh, I was thinking how very good life is. I'm so very happy, Babe. Looking forward to each new day as a challenge, wondering how I could be any happier, then discovering that every day brings more joy. We've got a gold mine, you know."

He pulled me close. "Yes, I know, sweetheart. And I'm convinced that we are going to make it and so are all these kids, problems and all." We got up, exhausted from the activities of the day. As Linnie unplugged the lights on the tree, I reached down and picked up an overlooked ornament, lying by the sofa.

"And here is our contribution to the first Christmas in our new life." As I placed it on the tree, we stood for just a moment, holding each other close, reluctant to leave the beauty we were sharing. As we turned to go, I heard Eddie and Lin laughing in their room. "Yes," I thought, "We are all going to make it!"

The next morning, I awoke suddenly, jarred by a loud noise. "Linnie, what's that?" I shook him awake, and he listened for a moment. "It's just the boys. Sounds like they're building a fire."

"But, it's in the middle of the night!"

"Sweetheart, it's 4:30 a.m. We planned to get up this early, remember? I have to leave for work at 6:30."

I sprang from bed, struggling to keep my eyes open, and grabbed my robe. "I'll call the kids while you dress."

Linnie laughed. "I don't think you'll have to. It sounds like they all beat us up."

As I hurried through the kitchen I passed Polly, fully dressed. "You'd better hurry", she smiled. "We're all getting impatient.. I'm getting the camera", and she continued on down the hall.

I could feel the warmth of the fire even before I entered the den. Eddie and Lin had already hauled wood and had it stacked against the hearth. Lin looked up as I entered. "That should be enough wood to hold us for a while", he said, wiping sawdust from his hands.

Mark and Janet both sat sleepily in front of the fire, staring at the mountain of presents waiting to be opened. Someone had turned on a radio, and Christmas carols pealed out into the den.

Linnie appeared in the doorway. "Is everybody here? Lin, you and Eddie be Santa for us. Everyone find a place and sit down. Come here Janet, here's a place by Momma and me."

Janet timidly eased over by Linnie and me, her face suddenly wrinkled by a very sleepy yawn. I reached over and pulled her hair out of her eyes and clipped it back as Lin and Eddie began to call out our names.

Twenty minutes later the den floor was covered with crunched paper, ribbons, boxes and gifts. One by one the kids came over and said "Thanks, Momma, thanks Daddy, for everything. It's a great Christmas.

As we gathered around the table for breakfast later, I stopped Linnie before he returned thanks. "I think this is the greatest Christmas I've ever had. God has blessed all of us so much, I'd like to have sentence prayers for our grace."

We all joined hands around the table and gave our individual thanks to God. Janet and Mark were too timid to pray aloud, but everyone else took a turn. My heart swelled as I heard each of the children, in his own way, thank God for our family and for bringing us together.

As we finished eating, Lin spoke. "Momma, that was a super breakfast. To show my appreciation, I'm washing the dishes."

"Wow!" Polly shouted. "This is a switch."

"I've been deserted, "Eddie muttered, knowing Lin was drawing him to perform an undesirable task.

"Come on, brother," Lin urged, pulling Eddie from his chair. "We showed them how to trim the tree. Let's show them how the experts do dishes."

Linnie and I sat and talked for a few minutes before he left for work. I watched as all the kids cleaned the table and did the dishes, laughing and kidding one another. This was another of those moments - - a gem to be tucked away in my heart.

Chapter 12

KNOCK, KNOCK

Webster defines "communication" as "the interchange of thoughts, opinions, or information by speech or writing." This has been a magical word in our home and I believe it is one of the keys to our success as a family. No one knows the mixed emotions I felt as I began to realize the magnitude of this great task Linnie and I had accepted. I knew that his kids had accepted me, but would they ever feel close to me? Would they confide in me as a friend as well as a mother, or would they remain in their own little worlds, leaving me out of their conversations and their problems? I knew that without communication as a vital part of our family life, we would be in serious trouble.

These questions concerned me the first weeks in our new home, but I knew God would work this out just as He had worked out other problems during our engagement. I had always been very open and honest with my own three children and tried to always be available if one of them needed to talk. To be able to communicate with people is necessary if we are to get along with them; and children, no matter what age, are "people", although many times we tend to forget that fact. They have the same fears, hopes, joys, and sadness that we have as adults.

I found that the secret to keeping the lines of communication open between the children and me was just treating them like "people" whom I respected and dearly loved. I listened intently when one was telling of an experience at school and tried to enter into their conversation when I could, being careful not to dominate it. I began to ask opinions of the girls about my clothes or makeup. As we worked together in the kitchen, I noticed that Polly and Thea were including me in their talk of school activities, etc. My heart overflowed with joy as I moved into the lives of these children and also accepted into their hearts!

It is so vital to be your children's friend as well as parent, and I believe I can say that all eight of ours were always friends to Linnie and me. Linnie and I both had always been strict parents, and his kids were very close to him when we met. However, as happens in many homes, after we were married, "Mom" became the buffer between the children and their dad. They began to come to me with any request they had – permission to go somewhere, special permission for a late bedtime, etc., and I would present the request to Dad. This may sound medievel and archaic to some, but in our home Daddy was always "boss." Jesus said that a man is to be head of his home, and I was constantly re-affirming this to the children. They all knew that any request had to pass Dad. This does not mean that Dad rules as a tyrant, but simply that he is fulfilling a God-given responsibility. He never made a decision without first asking my opinion about the matter. If we ever disagreed on a matter, we never discussed it in front of the kids but in the privacy of our bedroom. Everyone in our home knew that Daddy had the last word. So, I became liaison for the children, a challenge which I accepted joyfully as I realized that the children were all beginning to confide in me.

Polly received an invitation to a party about three months before her sixteenth birthday. Since we did not allow the children to date until they were sixteen, it posed a problem. She came to me with the request that she be allowed to attend with an escort. Well, both Polly and I knew that if Daddy said sixteen, he meant sixteen, but I agreed to see what I could do. I was always careful to choose a good time to present a problem or a request to Linnie.

That's simply what I label "wifely psychology." We were eating out on a Friday night, as we did once a month, and I casually said, "Babe, when you are finished with your meal, I have something to ask you." Knowing how his new family had begun to operate, he asked, "Okay, who wants what?" After a very hasty "NO!", and then asking what I thought about it, he agreed for Polly to go. Needless to say, she was ecstatic when I told her, and I felt our family becoming just a little closer.

Lin was in his second year of college when he came home for a weekend, and I noticed he seemed pensive and quiet. Linnie and I had suspected for several months that Lin was dissatisfied with his chosen field and were praying that he would find the place that God wanted him to be. At this time Lin was a co-op student in Charleston, SC, working his way through Clemson University in Chemical Engineering. He graduated from high school with honors so we knew he had the ability to excel, but lately his grades had begun to drop. Linnie and I had both hinted several times that maybe he was in the wrong major, but on each occasion he would insist that he liked it. We knew any decision made must be his and we didn't want to influence him.

Linnie had already gone to bed, and I was making a final check of the doors to make sure they were locked when Lin came into the kitchen. "Mom, can we talk for a few minutes?" Well, I was very tired after a long day and it was late, but I felt that this was more important than sleep right then. So, we sat down in the den and I listened as he told of his plans to quit school and join the Navy. I was shocked at his proposal to quit college but was careful not to let it show as I sat quietly while he talked. He told me of a friend he had met while working in Charleston who had just retired from a career in the Navy. This friend painted a very bright picture of the numerous opportunities and benefits of a Navy career. After Lin finished, he asked, "What do you think?" Well, to put it bluntly, I thought he was making a big mistake. But he didn't need for me to tell him that. He needed encouragement. I said, "Lin, have you prayed about this decision?" "No, Ma'am, not yet", he sighed, evidently weary from the mental strain he was under. I said, "Then, I think you should pray about it. God may not want all of his children to finish college, but I believe he does have a definite plan for each of us, including you." If you will seriously, unselfishly pray about this decision, seeking God's will and not yours, Daddy and I will support you in whatever you decide to do. We love you and want you to be happy because this is <u>YOUR</u> life and we can't live it for you. Just be sure it's what God wants. We will be much in prayer also that God will reveal His will to you. Don't rush into anything. Just take your time and talk it over with God."

I was deeply touched that Lin would confide in me with his problem since he and his dad were very close and he highly respected Linnie's wisdom and judgement.

The thought had occurred to me, as the children began to turn to me sometimes, that Linnie may resent my closeness to them, especially since his children had always confided in him before our marriage. But that's one of the many great things I've discovered about my husband and about our marriage. He is very understanding and unselfish and has always respected my ability to handle most situations that arise concerning the children. When Lin came to me with his problem about college, I was afraid that his dad may be hurt. Feeling totally spent but relieved that Lin's dilemma had surfaced, I told him goodnight and went to bed. Linnie was lying in bed reading, but as I entered the room, he laid his book down.

"Is one of the kids having a problem?" he asked.

"Not exactly". With a hesitant sigh I climbed into bed beside him and related our conversation in the den, not knowing how Linnie would take the news of Lin giving up college.

"Well, it's his life, sweetheart. As you said, it's got to be his decision. I'm sure he'll make the right one."

Then, as we settled down for the night, Linnie's arms encircled me and he tilted my head up and looked into my eyes, smiling.

"Well, Mom, that should at least prove you've really been accepted. He came to you with his problem, seeking your advice. It looks like we've really made it!"

Lin did leave college in June with plans to enlist in the Navy the following January. He got a job at a local grocery store as a meat cutter and seemed to be happy with his decision. Little did I know that God was dealing with him all this time. In late fall he left for a weekend to visit Eddie who was a freshman at Clemson University. On Sunday night after he returned home, he informed Linnie and me of his decision to re-enter school in January in another field of study. After changing majors, Lin was supremely happy in his chosen major of poultry science, graduated with honors and a commission of 2nd Lieutenant in the ROTC. Yes, I am convinced that God led Lin all the way. Sometimes He leads us through the forest, where it seems very dark and gloomy, in order for us to reach the open field where the light of His will shines as bright as the sun. (And who knows? Someday Lin may just need that experience he gained cutting meat!)

I told a friend once jokingly, "If you ever want privacy, don't live in a house with eight kids!" It seemed that before I left for work in the morning at least four or five of them needed me for something, and at night when I arrived home, it was worse. There is something magnetic about a closed door, too. It seemed that any time I would close my bedroom door, several minutes later I'd hear a knock. One night was especially busy after a very trying day at the office. Cindy had a problem she wanted to talk about and we talked about 20-25 minutes after supper when there was another knock. Mark said, "When you get through with Cindy, I want to talk with you about something." A little irritated, I replied, "Come back in five minutes, Mark." He was gently knocking again in five minutes. (Mark is very insistent.) Cindy went out and Mark entered and said "When I get through, there are two more waiting in line to talk to you." Well, that is a sample of the communication we had in our home.

My door may have been closed but the children knew that it was never closed to shut them out. For the day that I shut them out may be the day they cease coming to me and may seek out someone else. Each knock brought a new challenge. I never knew whether one had a crisis or just wanted to share an experience. And sharing is a vital part of parenthood – whether it is a joyful experience or a very sad and traumatic one. What may seem trivial and unimportant to us adults may be very meaningful to a young person.

Cindy came to me one night, saying she had a problem at school. A girl was talking about her on campus. Cindy was very upset and I could sense a slight animosity toward this girl as she spoke. I tried to comfort her, explaining that this young girl may have a bad home environment, may be a little jealous, or may be simply unhappy in life. I told Cindy to respond with kindness, to maintain a spirit of love, and to pray for her. I urged Cindy not to harbor ill feelings towards the girl, to forgive her, and seek the Lord for direction. She appeared to feel much better after our talk, and I asked her to let me know how things turned out. Several months later Cindy came to my room one night with a smile on her face.

"Mom, I think it's working with the girl at school."

"And how did it work out with your being nice to her and giving her love instead of animosity".

"Well, I prayed for her to like me and I have tried hard to be nice and smile at her when we pass at school. Today when I was leaving campus for the day, she smiled and said, 'Bye, Cindy."

I hugged her close and said, "See how much better things work out when we do it God's way?"

I could see the look of real accomplishment on her face and knew that God had blessed her abundantly that day.

As adults we would probably not give a situation like this a second thought, but to Cindy it was paramount. And since it was real to her, that made it extremely important to me. This is what communication is-listening, really listening. And offering advice with wisdom sought from the Holy Spirit. With effective communication, most problems can be discussed and resolved.

There came a time when I had to face the fact that unless I took definite steps, I would never have complete privacy for a prolonged period. If I was in the middle of my Bible study time or trying to write, invariably someone would knock on the bedroom door. So I printed a sign which read "MEDITATING – DO NOT DISTURB" and explained to all of the kids why I was using it. Then, if they came to my door and saw the sign posted, they all knew that only an emergency gave them the right to knock. It gave me some valuable time for myself and ultimately taught them many times to make decisions for themselves.

The talks weren't always originated by the children. There were many "conferences" (The kids called them "conferences" when Linnie or I initiated them) held in our bedroom with one who may have been having a specific problem which may have been a source of friction, or unhappiness within our home, etc. I believe that all of the children can say they have had several "conferences" with me or Linnie or both of us together. We later learned that it sometimes became a joke among the children when they were called for a meeting. If Linnie sent word to the den for one to come to our room, I could hear them all teasing, "Uh, Oh, what did _you_ do?"

We always made it a habit not to infringe upon the privacy of any of our children, and we expected the same from them. When the girls began dating, we never asked how serious they were about a boy, where they went on a date, etc. As people, they were entitled to their lives and their decisions. We always requested to know something about the boys the girls dated and beyond that their privacy was respected unless they overstepped set bounds. When each of the children went out the first time, I would talk with them about respect and how the girls should demand respect from any boy they dated. When I talked with the boys, I would tell them to always respect the girls they dated as if the girl was their sister. And I told all of the kids, "Just remember _who_ you are, and _whose_ you are. You belong to Jesus, and you should act as He would."

In rare cases they did make foolish decisions and were

disciplined for them, and some did not understand the discipline at the time. But they did seem to understand it as coming from parents who loved them and cared what happened to them. If children understand and can compare those rules with the rules God sets for us as his children, then our children will love us more dearly for each rule. I always reminded our children that God sometimes chastens us when we disobey, not because he likes to punish but because he loves us so much and wants us to be more like Jesus. This is communication!

Our children had the privacy of their rooms and this was their own private world. Neither Linnie nor I ever entered a closed room without knocking and being invited in. We started our home in this manner and the children really appreciated it. We requested the same right to our privacy. Once or twice the young ones would burst into our room without knocking and were reprimanded for it. The last time Mark did that to me, he found me just getting out of the bath. I don't think we ever had to remind *him* again. Even when one girl wished to enter another girl's room, she knocked to be invited in. This is courtesy for another person – this is the golden rule in action. This is communication!

We laugh together, we cry together, and we sometimes hurt together, but we communicate – and that's the important thing!

Chapter 13

THE DEER STAND DEBACLE

I discussed with Linnie at length Mark's diagnosis of ADHD. Mark needed additional reassurance and support following the death of his biological father. However, Linnie thought once we got Mark into the country atmosphere of our new home, any problems would be resolved. Mark was doing fifth grade work when tested, but he was failing in third grade. Conflicts kept arising between Mark and Linnie after we settled in Norway. One day when Mark was about eleven, he came to the den door and called out excitedly, "Mom, come quick! I want to show you something." I immediately thought something was wrong.

"Not again," I thought as I dried my hands from washing vegetables.

"What is it, Mark?"

"Just come and see", he called out.

I followed him out the door and around the corner of the house. There, leaning against the pecan tree, was a very crudely built ladder with around five or six rungs in it.

"I built this for Daddy", he smiled, still excited. "He can use it to get up in the tree stand to hunt deer. Do you think he will like it? Do you, Mom?"

"Mark, you sure did a good job. I'll bet Daddy will be proud of you. But, did you ask him if you could use the tools you had to borrow for the job and for the wood you used?"

Mark hung his head for a moment, his excitement dampened.

"No, Ma'am. But I bet he won't mind after he sees what a good job I did."

He quickly dismissed my concern. Later after supper was over that night, Mark couldn't contain himself any longer.

"Daddy, come and see what I did for you!", Mark cried out, running out the door. Linnie and I followed close behind him to the shop where all the tools were kept.

"See, Daddy, I built you a deer ladder to get up to the tree stand!"

For several moments Linnie didn't comment at all. Then I noticed his face turning a deeper shade of red as he lashed out.

"And who gave you permission to go in my shop and use my tools, young man?" His voice got louder as he lost his temper. "You can just get the hammer and take every piece of wood apart and put it back on the wood stacked in the shop. And don't touch my tools ever again without asking first!"

Mark's face mirrored the shock that was in his heart. He couldn't say a word. But I could see the brokenness in his spirit. Disillusioned and crushed, he stood there in unbelief with tears spilling out over his cheeks.

"Linnie!" I cried out to him. "Mark realized that he didn't ask permission. Just try to see the good job that he did."

The unbidden tears coursed down my cheeks as I turned and ran inside the house. Linnie followed closely behind. When he came up the steps and inside the den, I could tell that he was still furious.

"You can have it. All of it - - the house, the land, everything. I can't do this anymore! he shouted." The mounting tensions and stress Linnie felt in filling the daunting role of being Daddy to eight children were exploding right before my eyes. He was shaking and turned to walk away in exasperation.

"Oh, Linnie, I don't believe you just said that. I just can't believe it!" The tears continued to flow as I covered my face with my hands.

Linnie's anger gave way to reason, and he immediately looked at me with brokenness and regret. "Oh, sweetheart, I am so sorry, so very sorry. I didn't mean what I just said."

Linnie came over and dropped down on his knees beside me. "Please forgive me, please. I didn't mean anything I just said. What can I do to undo what just happened?" His eyes were pleading with me.

"I forgive you, Linnie. But all of our children witnessed this scene. They are probably scared to death and can't imagine what this means. I want you to call all of them together and apologize to them so that their minds might be somewhat relieved.

"I'll do anything, anything. Sweetheart, just stop crying." He left my side and began to call the children. Most of them had been standing near the den, and they had heard everything that was said.

"I want you kids to know that I am deeply sorry for what I just said. I was just reacting with anger. I assure you that your mom and I are going to stick with this marriage no matter what might happen. Mark, I am sorry for the way I reacted toward your attempt to please me. Please forgive me."

Both of us hugged all of the children that were present and assured them that we loved them greatly. All of the kids gave Linnie grace after this experience. Emotionally drained from the ordeal, Linnie couldn't understand at the time that he especially needed Mark's forgiveness. We healed, as a family, following this painful experience, and I don't believe the episode was spoken of again until many years later.

Things got better, even though there were strained feelings for some time between Mark and his dad. Today, Mark and Linnie converse regularly, and have admiration and respect for each other. Sometimes incredibly hard experiences help us to grow and learn how to give grace, forgive, and lean more on our heavenly Father.

Chapter 14

PRIVILEGES EARNED

One day after Thea left for college, I came home from work tired as usual, hoping that I wouldn't have a crisis at home. Things had been going pretty well lately with Polly now in charge. Lin and Eddie were established at Clemson University and Thea was progressing in her studies to become a Laboratory Technologist. She was still living at home and working part-time to help pay for expenses in school.

When I came in the back door, Polly met me. My pocketbook in hand, I was relishing the thought of sitting in my room in silence for a few, brief moments.

"Mom, Julie and Cindy haven't done the clothes this afternoon," Polly stated.

"I have had to remind them every day, but the clothes still aren't getting folded and put away. I know you don't need an extra worry, but I have been unable to solve this problem by myself. I really hesitate to tell Daddy about it, because I know he will be hard on both of them."

I went into my room, closed the door, and sat down on the side of the bed. I needed to handle this latest problem and couldn't face it in my own strength. I heaved a sigh, and looked up to heaven.

"Father, I am struggling here," I prayed. "I don't know how to go forward. I don't want to punish Julie and Cindy, but I can't think how to get through to them that they have to pull their weight in our household. I need your strength and your wisdom in this matter. Let me know how to approach them without harshness."

I sat still and quiet and just listened for that still, small voice of God that guided me every day. God didn't answer audibly, but I somehow knew how to move forward without seeming so strict with the girls. I got up and immediately got a piece of typing paper and wrote on it in magic marker, "PRIVILEGES COME WITH RESPONSIBILITY". I went through the kitchen and told Polly to hold supper while I talked with Julie and Cindy.

"Good luck!" she replied. I taped the sign on the girl's bedroom door and then knocked.

"Come in", Julie said.

"Girls, I want to talk to both of you for a few minutes before supper," I began. "I think you probably know what it is about. Polly told me that you haven't been doing your part in our family recently to help us pull together. The clothes haven't been folded before I get home. Julie, do you remember how you have been complaining lately that the older girls get to go places and do things that you and Cindy don't get to do? I've been reminding you both that Lin and Eddie get to do things that Polly and Thea don't get to do. Privileges come with responsibility! If you younger girls show that you can be responsible for doing your chores around the house, you will be given more privileges. Polly has jobs around the house, and those chores are done consistently. And she in turn gets to enjoy outings and other rewards. Your job is to help with laundry, to fold the clothes, and then deliver the clothes to each person's bedroom. Do you girls understand what I am saying?"

Cindy and Julie both nodded their heads. "Yes Ma'am", they said in unison.

"So, Dad and I will be looking to see that the clothes are done. And done without anyone reminding you to do your job. Then, you will enjoy added privileges. It won't be long before you, Julie, will have to get in the kitchen to help Polly with kitchen detail. Polly has a big responsibility on her shoulders, and you younger girls can be a big help to her. Now, how about getting these clothes folded and delivered so we can all eat together. I'd really rather not have to bring this matter to Daddy when he gets home!"

Later that evening as Julie and Cindy walked into their room at bedtime, they both tapped the sign I'd put on the door. Before saying goodnight, Julie stepped forward and cleared her voice to get my attention.

"Ahem."

I glanced towards Julie, and saw a smile spread across her face. I smiled back and said, "Goodnight, girls!"

"Goodnight, Mom."

Leaning my head back and breathing a sigh of relief, I closed my eyes. I was so tired. But refreshed. And thankful for God's still, small voice leading me through another dilemma.

"You okay," Linnie asked?

"Yeah, I'm okay." My eyes opened and I looked his way. He reached for my hand, and a calming peace fell over me.

"No, I'm not okay. I'm great."

We sat in the den together talking about the children, Linnie's day at work, and what we'd do the coming weekend. Weary but renewed, we left the den for bed, and night turned into another day.

Things began to get better after my talk with the girls about chores. Julie and Cindy eventually assumed cooking duties after Polly left for nursing school, and could prepare any kind of meal I left on the menu. I was so proud of them! In addition, Julie helped Linnie outside with yard chores, and Cindy helped me on the weekends prepare many different dishes for our big Sunday lunch. Oh, and by the way, I never had to mention the incident to Linnie!

Chapter 15

Rules, A Necessity

Before Linnie and I got married, we discussed how we would manage with ten people in one house without major problems. After the wedding and merger of the two families, we called all of the children together and informed them there would be certain rules in our home so that we would have a semblance of order. Countries are founded on rules and guidelines for order. A family is no exception.

Every school morning the kids would be called two by two because we only had two bathrooms. If you missed getting up and dressed and to the breakfast table, you missed breakfast and went to school hungry. It only happened once or twice with the kids but after missing breakfast, it didn't happen again. Linnie and I had kitchen detail in the morning. He would get up earlier than I did and put the grits on. Then I would join him in the kitchen and finish up breakfast. Thea and Polly helped get the table set and checked on Janet and Mark, the youngest ones.

Most of the kids took their showers at night, and they were only allowed fifteen minutes for their shower time. I'm sure they felt like they were in the armed services, but with only two bathrooms for ten people, these rules were a neccessity.

Each child was required to get a job when they were sixteen, with no exceptions. They had to learn the responsibility of tithing, of putting up a certain amount for college or to help with family expenses, and how to handle their money.

The girls were not allowed to wear makeup until they were sixteen, except for a small amount of blush and lipstick. I was in the kitchen one morning when Julie and Cindy came through to go to school. I stopped them short.

"And where do you think you both are going, with all of that eye make-up and mascara? The rule is: no heavy makeup until sixteen. That doesn't mean fourteen. A little bit of blush and a little bit of lip gloss. All of you kids heard Daddy spell out the rules for you." Cindy was tempted to balk, but she knew I was right. Turning around with a huff, she returned to her room. Julie followed with heavy steps and her shoulders down. A few minutes later they returned, radiant and beautiful. Not happy with our rule, but compliant nonetheless.

We had some trouble with the mode of dress as it pertained to our girls. Fads come and fads go, but it seemed that our girls followed every fad that "came down the pike." I remembered a saying of my mother's, "You'd better pick your battles or you'll have real trouble." For the most part, I let the girls alone with their stacked, platform shoes, low riding jeans, and jeans that dragged the floor. If they ever came out of their rooms with short shorts on, I simply turned them around to redress.

The telephone rules didn't go over real well with the kids, but were necessary with a large family with several people wanting to make or receive calls. Linnie set ten minutes for each call. The girls didn't appreciate our phone call limits especially when they started dating. We even had to set a timer a couple of times. After the girls were engaged, Linnie made some exceptions and extended the phone call times.

Today, everyone has a cell phone, and it would be near impossible to limit phone usage. But parents would be wise to make some rules about cell phone usage during family times, especially during meals. And to regularly check cell activity. It is your responsibility, parents, to monitor phone usage, text messaging, and social media activity as much as possible.

Our children weren't allowed to date until they were sixteen, and then only once a week. I firmly agree with documented studies stating that adolescents differ from adults in the way they behave, solve problems, and make decisions. Research shows that brains continue to mature and develop throughout childhood and adolescence and well into adulthood. How can we as parents expect teenagers to make rational decisions, to read social and behavioral cues and act appropriately, or pause to consider the consequences of their actions when their minds are still developing? Limiting the time our children could spend with the opposite sex and setting limits on the dating age was a rule Linnie and I felt very strongly about. We discouraged the children from getting serious at an early age. Dating gave our sons and daughters an excellent opportunity to widen their friendships. And develop more serious relationships as they grew and matured. Linnie and I always required to know something about the boy before our daughters accepted a date. All the girls were respectful of our wishes and they almost always asked permission before accepting a first date. Julie was a senior engaged to be married after graduation and still dated only once a week. Our boys never dated in high school by choice.

I was talking to a friend one day about the perils of teenagers dating.

"I don't know what I am going to do", she said. I worry so much about my daughter dating so steady. She insists on going with only one boy and sees him almost every day. If she isn't at his house, he's at mine. How in the world do you manage to keep your girls' dating to a minimum?

"It's really quite simple. Linnie and I make the rules. But then we go a step further, a step many parents fail to take. We explain to the girls why the rule has been made. In the matter of dating, I explained to all of my girls why we only want them to date once a week and why we don't allow them to date until they are sixteen.

Most of the time when we explain the reason behind a rule, the kids understand. Even when adhering to the rule is hard, the girls accept our final word. Because it is final. And when it's all said and done, the children know we love them above all else."

I'm sure Julie felt that we were being unfair when she became engaged and was still allowed only one date a week. I sat down one day and had a long talk with her, explaining the dangers of heavy dating and the temptations she would face, especially during a long engagement. I also had a similar talk with her fiance; we explained our reasons for trying to keep them both from becoming too involved emotionally and physically. They both accepted our decision with understanding and seemed to appreciate our concern.

Sixteen was a gigantic milestone at our house for our young people. Not only were they allowed to drive at night when they reached sixteen, but they were also allowed to date. I'm sure we were in the minority making our kids wait until they were sixteen to date, but it paid off. They had this to look forward to while establishing and cultivating friendships. In addition, it protected them from being put in possibly compromising situations before they were mature enough to make rational, well thought-out decisions.

Cindy came to me one day when she was fifteen to complain about the rule "no dating until sixteen". She had a cousin who was dating at fourteen. "Mom, everybody else is dating at fourteen or fifteen. I don't see why we have to wait." I took a few minutes out from my work and tried to explain.

"Look at it this way, Honey. If you date, go where you want, do all this at fourteen, what is there for you to anticipate at fifteen or sixteen? You would have to have new and bigger thrills, more excitement. Things you did at fourteen or fifteen would be "the pits" as you kids say. Situations you can't handle at fourteen you'll be better prepared for at sixteen or seventeen. When you do reach sixteen and begin to date, you'll be better able to understand what I mean, and I feel like you'll be glad you waited."

I'm not sure she accepted all I said then, but I do know she felt better about why Linnie and I made the rule. I still feel that after she began to date at sixteen, she was glad she had waited.

I was asked the question many times while we were rearing our children, "Why don't your kids rebel against your strict rules and curfews?" The only answer I had to give them is that all of our children knew the rules were made because we loved them and wanted only the best for them. They were also told the reasons for each rule and they usually accepted our way as best. Since Christ is the center and ruler of our home, the kids knew that He commands from children honor and respect for parents and they obeyed that command. Someone said to me once when we began our new home and established these rules, "I think you're being too strict with your kids. Time will tell." Well, time was on our side, and I can say truthfully that after raising eight kids for twenty years none of them has given us any serious trouble. They all grew into responsible adults who revered God, knew how to respect others, and demonstrated a strong work ethic. I think that record speaks for itself!

Work outside the home was necessary for all of our young people. We gave the children a small allowance for jobs done around the house. But as soon as they were able they secured outside jobs and were encouraged to tithe and to put aside a certain amount of their money. The older boys were working when Linnie and I got married, and it wasn't long before the girls began to seek employment. Before they could hold a public job at sixteen, they would baby sit, pick vegetables for the surrounding farmers or work at odd jobs to earn money.

Several years our pecan trees bore a large crop of pecans. The kids picked up nuts, shelled them, and sold the bagged pecans to earn money for clothes. One summer Mark arose many mornings at 5:00 a.m. to pick cantaloupes. He earned over $300 and bought most of his school clothes that year. Janet, being a younger girl, wasn't allowed to work in the fields as much, but she earned a good bit and helped purchase some winter clothes as well. Cindy and Julie also did babysitting, and worked to earn money as young teenagers. Cindy was called first to a grocery store when she reached sixteen.

Cindy was always very shy and unsure of herself in any endeavor, and this new experience was no exception. I noticed she was extremely nervous the first day when I put her out at the store. "I'll pick you up this afternoon, Hon. You'll be great. I will pray for you." When I picked her up, her face told me what she didn't have to say - - she was disillusioned. We didn't speak during the ride home because I knew if she spoke the flood of tears she was struggling to hold back would come and all the other kids in our home would see her. When we reached home, I called her into my room.

"Okay, let's have it, Hon," I said softly. What happened?" That was all it took to burst the dam. The sobs came and for a few minutes I stood silently and let her cry into my shoulder. Then I tried to calm her. "Tell me what happened, Cindy."

"Mom, I can't do it. I just can't!" she almost screamed at me, the tears still streaming. "I can't figure the amounts right. Sometimes it's 6 cans for $1.00. We have to figure it fast. You know how bad I am at math." The excuses kept pouring out between sobs. "I'm not going back. I'll call them now and tell them. I'm too dumb to learn all that. I can't make change right. I can't figure the prices in my head," her body jerked with sobs. "I just can't go back, Mom. Please don't make me."

I knew the worst thing for her was to quit this job. If I allowed her to quit, to give up, she would find it easier to quit the next one, and the next. One of the most difficult jobs I've ever had as a parent was to be firm and resolute in my decision to her right then.

My heart went out to her because I could remember my first public job. I was only thirteen, very shy and unsure of myself. Her feelings weren't so different from mine then, but I knew it wouldn't help her to tell her that.

"You will not quit this job, Cindy. You will go back at 9:00 a.m. tomorrow and try again. If they tell you that you are incapable of performing the job, then you can quit. But until then you will report to work as scheduled. You've accepted the job, they have invested time in your training, and you will not give up so easily. You know I've always told you kids not to give up on something, but to see it through. So, dry your eyes, get something to eat, and make up your mind you can do it."

I believe that's the nearest Cindy has ever come to feeling hate towards me. I almost hated myself for my firmness. She wiped her tear-stained face and swollen eyes and left the room without speaking. In fact, she didn't speak to me anymore that day. As I recall, she went to bed early.

I prayed that night that God would grant her understanding and give her the self-assurance she so desperately needed to conquer this job.

The next morning we drove in silence to the store. When I stopped to let her out, I reached over and touched her hand. "Cindy, I know you probably hate me right now. But three or four months from now you'll understand and will probably be glad I made you try again. Just do the best you can today and remember I'll be praying for you all morning."

I choked back the tears as she mutely got out of the car and walked into the store without a word. As I drove out of the parking lot and headed home, the tears flowed as I cried out to God. "Please, Lord Jesus, be with Cindy and guide her, calm her and help her through this. Keep your hand on her shoulder and let her know You are there. Help her to know that I love her. Please don't let her hate me."

I continued to send prayers up to God all morning on behalf of Cindy. Every time I thought about her at the register, struggling with her feelings, I prayed. Waiting for her outside the store at 12:00, I was filled with apprehension. When she came through the door, I thought I detected a slight spring in her step, a look of accomplishment that wasn't there the day before.

"How'd it go?" I asked in a calm tone.

"Figuring the prices is hard and making change is still hard. But it wasn't as bad as yesterday, Mom." I felt ten feet tall then because I knew she was going to make it. I knew she already partially understood why I wouldn't let her give up. Silently, I said, "Thank you, Jesus!"

For the next two nights on the den floor surrounded by nickels, dimes, pennies and quarters, we made change. I was the customer, and Cindy was the clerk. We even made a joke out of it to suppress any tension she felt. I was sometimes an irate customer when she made a mistake. "What's the matter, Young Lady? You don't know how to figure prices?" I would say. "Cool it, Ma'am," she would say smiling. I'll get it right in a minute. Just don't get uptight." I made signs with prices, i.e., 3/69 cents, 2/39 cents, 4/98 cents, etc., and drilled her until she knew them without hesitating.

Each day I could see her attitude improving, the dread disappearing as she readied for work. Three months after she began working she got a raise which boosted her ego. We were talking one day and she said, "You know, Mom, every time I think about changing jobs something happens to change my mind. I've been seriously considering it lately, and yesterday the assistant bookkeeper said I was the most accurate checker in the store. My register checked perfect when they did a surprise audit last Saturday night." Somehow, I felt the time was right to ask. "Aren't you glad now that I wouldn't let you quit that first day?" She smiled wide, braces shining. "Yes, Ma'am." That one smile made it all worthwhile.

The family altar was begun in our home several months after our family had married. We established it to begin at 9:00 p.m., right before the children were required to be in their rooms. They balked at first but after several weeks, the kids agreed with us that we all needed a closer walk with our Lord Jesus, and they never complained again.

If our kids could give their testimony here, I believe they would all say that they are glad they were always required to accept responsibility, to work for their clothes, and to help out at home.

All children need to be given responsibility from a very early age in order for them to grow into responsible adults who can contribute to our society.

As the older kids graduated and left for college, we had to "shift" jobs and rearrange our schedule. When Thea and Polly left home, Julie and Cindy moved into the kitchen, Janet inherited the clothes, and Mark's responsibilities broadened with the farm chores and wood cutting. All the girls learned by trial and error the techniques of cooking. It hasn't always been easy for them or me. Some of them grumbled about cooking, and many times it would have been easier for me to do it myself; but with perseverance all of the girls could prepare a full meal when they left home.

Many times friends have asked me "How do you possibly manage with eight children?" The secret - - organization. If any group or business is to function it must be organized - - and we are in the business of having a happy, healthy home. When our college kids came home for the holidays and vacations, we always had to sit down as a family and discuss our schedule and ask everybody to cooperate. I realized that it wasn't easy for those who had been away to come back into a regimented schedule, to conform to our rules, but, for the most part, they cooperated. They seemed to understand that in order to operate the family smoothly, we had to operate as a team.

The first time Lin came home from college he got up at 6:00 a.m. to take his shower, not realizing that we called the school kids at the same time. When I glanced down the hall from the kitchen, I saw four of the children standing by the bathroom door, waiting to get in. After I explained the problem with Lin, the problem never arose again.

I know that there have been times when the kids felt that we were being unfair. There were probably times when they felt that we were placing too much responsibility on them. But through the years, I have seen all eight of them grow and develop into responsible, unselfish adults, fully capable of running the home if Linnie and I were called away.

Several years after we were married, Linnie suffered a ruptured disc and was in the hospital in Columbia for surgery. He was admitted on Tuesday and scheduled for surgery on Thursday. It was right after Christmas so all of the college kids were home in addition to our two foster children. I knew I couldn't leave him for several days after surgery because he had to be turned every two hours.

The night before he was admitted I called all of the kids together and told them of my dilemma, soliciting their help. I made out menus, assigned duties for each one and confidently left the house in their hands. I was sure that with their training, the task wouldn't be too great for them. Well, the girls proved themselves extremely capable, preparing meals for ten, handling the heavy wash, and caring for our two little ones.

I came home on Saturday to help with clean-up and help prepare Sunday dinner, to find that the house had been cleaned, the wash done, and Sunday dinner already planned. The kids all promptly sent me to bed to get some much needed rest, assuring me everything was under control. At times like this I was glad we required the children to accept responsibility and learn how to function as a team in a crisis. My heart swelled with pride, and I felt a calm assurance that our labors were not in vain.

For a while after Linnie and I were married, we had only one television in our home. We all gathered in the den where we would agree on watching a program. There were certain programs the kids were not allowed to watch. Dad or I would put our okay on any new program they may have wanted to watch. The soap operas in the afternoon were off limits. One day when I returned home from work, I had a feeling Cindy and Julie were watching soap operas. I came into the den and put my hand on the television set and it was warm. I surmised that it had been on for quite a while. The girls reluctantly admitted to watching afternoon soap operas while I was away. And then we had to have a discussion about rules, consequences, values, and being mindful about how Satan can invade their thoughts and actions through entertainment. As parents, we have the responsibility to voice our standards to our children and to lead them by example. I don't think we ever had that problem again.

Parents, we are charged with raising our children in the admonition of the Lord. With much prayer and consideration of each child's unique personality, needs, and temperament, we must seek God to place some restraints and rules on our offspring. Rise to the occasion, and regulate your children's activities! Then your home will become a place of order, peace, and refuge, even during the troublesome teenage years!

Our eight wonderful children have made an "impossible" task not only possible but a beautiful journey of learning for them and for us! *"For whom the Lord loves he corrects, even as a father loves the son in whom he delights."* (Proverbs 3:11-12) God's words of wisdom which have never let us down.

Chapter 16

WELCOME, STRANGERS

After four of our children entered college, you would have thought I'd savor the time with less children at home. Well, I did for a short while. But, the Lord had other plans for us. At church one Sunday, I noticed a picture of a young boy on the front of the bulletin. The story featured a child named Kenny at Connie Maxwell Children's Home. Kenny was a candidate for adoption. Hours after church, I could not get his image out of my mind. That evening, I approached Linnie, and asked if we could talk.

"Linnie, I've been thinking about this boy on the bulletin all afternoon. I can't get him out of my head," I said.

"Wait a minute. You don't want to adopt him, do you?" Linnie asked.

"No, I wasn't thinking along those lines," I answered. "I was thinking we could have him come visit us for the holidays."

A complete look of relief fell over Linnie's face.

"We've already raised four good kids who will be responsible adults. I'd like to share what we have with someone else," I said. "Even though it will be hard. And exhausting. The children who are at home will have to agree to this."

"Are you sure this is what you want?" Linnie questioned. "If you really feel strongly about doing this, then I'm all for it."

"Why don't we pray about this now. We don't have to make this decision tonight."

So, we prayed together in our bedroom, asking God to show us His will. And I prayed again before bedtime, wondering what plan God was orchestrating for us.

Several days later, our hearts were both leaning towards inviting this precious child into our home. One night we approached Julie, Cindy, Mark, and Janet about our imminent plans. We explained to them that they would have to help carry the load of household chores. And that having Kenny may not always be easy. The children listened intently, and all unanimously agreed to the plan.

I was ecstatic! The next day, I made the phone calls to Connie Maxwell, and we soon drove to Greenwood for interviews and to fill out the necessary paperwork. We drove home, excited but also apprehensive about this new experience soon to happen.

When the time came, we traveled to Connie Maxwell as a family to bring Kenny home for Thanksgiving. It didn't take long for Kenny to fit right in with our routines, rules, and house rhythms.

Kenny eventually spent several summers, Thanksgiving and Christmas vacations with us and got along well with the kids who were still at home. We loved him, yet discipled him as if he were our own. He responded warmly to us! And we could see a gradual change in his demeanor. Once sullen and guarded, Kenny blossomed into a smiling, lovable young man.

Even though having an added child in our home WAS hard, I knew God was honoring our obedience to His will. And God's will brought us an abundance of joy! Kenny eventually graduated from Connie Maxwell, and entered the armed forces. We received a Christmas card from Kenny a few years ago. He wrote about how much he enjoyed staying with us in our home. In the card was a picture of Kenny, all grown up and so handsome.

Polly was currently in college training to be a registered nurse. Thea was in clinical training at a nearby college. Julie and Cindy were the oldest kids at home, along with Mark and Janet.

About this time, we received a call from Connie Maxwell, asking if we would again consider keeping two children who were four and six years old for approximately nine months. The administrator explained that the children needed prompt placement, that they had just been removed from their home. Linnie agreed with little hesitation, and the plans were soon in motion for us to gain these two young children.

Brenda and Winslow came into our home and into our hearts for nine months. I registered Winslow for first grade immediately after they arrived. These two precious children had never used indoor plumbing, would not eat at the table, and didn't know how to use a napkin. We taught them by example the first week. By the second week, they no longer used the rest room in the yard, and would sit at the table to eat meals. They were so frightened; it nearly broke my heart.

Winslow was an extremely quiet little boy. But, not Brenda! She was a precocious one. We never knew what she would say or how she would react to something that was said. Both of them were scared to death of Linnie and his rough, deep voice. They seemed to cling to me when he was around home.

Winslow was a small child with scraggly, brown hair which hung over one of his large, brown eyes. Brenda was large for her age with long, blond wavy hair which covered her frightened blue eyes. They looked more like twins because there was almost no difference in their height. Winslow was thin and Brenda, stocky.

We showed the children Polly and Thea's room where they would be sleeping. They stared at the twin beds and seemed to be shocked that they could sleep in a bed.

Little Brenda wet the bed every night. I would wash her linens each morning and hang them out to dry. Brenda followed me everywhere and would ask why I washed the sheets. On Friday I washed the linens from my own bed and Brenda asked, "Miss Annette, whose sheets 'dem is?"

"These are my sheets," I replied.

She looked up at me with a perplexed look and said, "You pee in the bed, too?" I laughed that day so hard my sides hurt. And every time I think of it now, I laugh again!

The days moved into weeks and the foster kids seemed to be adjusting beautifully to a routine in our household. They had to be taught to eat what was on the table at mealtimes though introducing a new food to them was a challenge. One night we had chili and it was a little spicy. Linnie had to constantly say, "Win, (our nickname for Winslow) eat your supper. You can't get down from the table until you finish eating. We didn't give you much."

Linnie went back to his meal. I sat across from Win and saw him scrunch his face up in a frown and make a fist in the air at Linnie. Linnie didn't see the gesture. But, I did! So did the other children. We all stifled our laughter, but thought it was hilarious!

Both of the children crammed food in their mouths as if it might be taken from them. This was another challenge for us. They also chewed with their mouths open. I had reminded them over and over again not to do this until they finally seemed to have mastered the art. Brenda and I were shopping one day and stopped to get a burger and coke for lunch. Brenda had been doing really good at keeping her mouth closed while eating. In the middle of our meal she suddenly spoke our loudly, "Look over there, Miss Annette. That man is chewing with his mouth wide open!" I could have slid under the table as I quieted her down.

"Well, she's getting it, God," I smiled.

Of course we took the children to church with us, but Win didn't adapt to church as well as Brenda did. Every Sunday morning when we got ready to go, Julie would say, "Mom, Win is hiding behind the sofa again." Linnie would have to go into the den and manually retrieve him from the sofa hiding place and get him to the car. After several Sundays of that behavior, Win began to enjoy the Bible lessons and stories and activities.

Julie, Cindy, Mark and Janet were the only kids left at home and they had the responsibility of keeping Brenda and Win when Linnie and I had to be away. I wasn't employed at this time, and was able to be at home when all of the children returned from school.

Things were going smoothly at home, and Linnie was now on day shift at work. He experienced extreme pain in his lower back. I had never seen anything keep Linnie from his job, or work on the farm. The doctors diagnosed him with a ruptured disc, scheduling him for therapy, and ultimately surgery. A friend of ours offered to keep Brenda during school hours for several days so I could be at the hospital to minister to Linnie. He recovered from the back surgery quickly and returned to work. However, three weeks later he pulled a muscle at work and had to be at home for an additional six weeks.

After school was out in May, Win and Brenda were returned to the custody of their father. We were thrilled that the children would be reunited with their dad. But, saying goodbye to them was a bittersweet time for all of us.

Our household became "normal" again with only six people to feed. What a change! No longer did we buy 10 pounds of bacon and 10 dozen eggs at one time. No longer did I have a sweet, little shadow following me around the house while the other children were at school. Their time with us came to a close, and I was thankful for every moment.

When Win and Brenda left us, they left with their very own Bibles which our church presented to them. I can still see them now. Standing proudly, clutching their white bibles, with bright smiles on their faces. I knew our lives would never be the same. They left with Bibles, and also with refreshed spirits. With lessons learned that will be with them forever.

Chapter 17

TRAIN UP A CHILD

"*T*rain up a child in the way he should go and when he is old, he will not depart from it.*" (Proverbs 22:6) In our home we wholeheartedly believed it, we lived it, and we practiced it daily. God entrusted these lives to us to be brought up *"in the nurture and admonition of the Lord"* (Ephesians 6:4). This is a big responsibility, the care, instruction, and discipline of children, a responsibility which too many parents treat lightly. It is a never-ending job, this "training up" of a child, a job that requires constant, 24-hour a day effort.

Rearing a child from birth to be a responsible, mature adult, able to assume his place in our world with confidence, is indeed a challenge. A formidable calling, but one of the most rewarding jobs two people can share. A husband and wife are given a life, a human being, to mold and shape until the finished product either stands tall as an asset to God and his family or is scorned by society as a liability to mankind. The end result will depend many times upon the dedication and faithfulness of those two people in charge of that life. "Training up a child" not only means moral and religious training, but other avenues of learning - - learning how to keep a clean room, learning to assume some responsibility at an early age, learning the beauty of the God-given gift of sex, I could go on and on. This job of training is a continuing thing, and the miracle is that the parents learn too. It's a joint venture.

When I "inherited" five extra lives to train, I was a little unsure of Linnie's philosophy regarding training children. I had observed Linnie's children in their home as well as mine, and was aware that they were given many tasks because of the circumstances of a one-parent home. I knew I was faced with a full-time job of training these special children to be responsible, hard working adults who also honored God.

Personal Responsibility

Anne Landers said *"It is not what you do for your children but what you have taught them to do for themselves that will make them successful human beings."* Our children learned early to keep their rooms tidy, and to make their beds before leaving for school in the morning. Cleanliness was stressed, and each was held responsible for his own linens. They all accepted responsibilities around the home and were each given specific chores to do. Sometimes the smaller ones didn't do a "blue-ribbon" job, but improvement came with time and patience. They were given small chores at first which were enlarged as they grew.

Saturday was our clean-up day. The older four girls took turns cleaning the bathrooms, dusting the den and living room and helping with the general cleaning. Each one of the kids had the responsibility of stripping his bed and vacuuming and dusting his own room. You can imagine what kind of cleaning a nine-year-old does, but I knew that Mark and Janet had to learn so they struggled through with my assurances that with patience and practice they could make a bed without one side of the spread hanging four inches on the floor.

Mark and Janet's first attempts at making their beds was a step short of a "disaster". Polly had been making Janet's bed, and before we moved there I had always had domestic help. With such a large family, I felt it was time that both of them shouldered the responsibility of their rooms. The first Saturday that I required them to be in charge of changing their linens and cleaning their rooms, they wanted to give up before either of them got started. I passed Janet's room on my way to pick up some clothes from Polly and Thea and heard Janet mumbling under her breath. Pausing for a moment to glance in, I saw her struggling with her spread, obviously much distressed and annoyed that this job was proving too much for her. When she suddenly caught sight of me in the doorway, she exclaimed, "Momma, I just can't do this. Nothing works right. The spread keeps moving around." She sank on the bed atop the crumpled spread in a spirit of utter defeat.

"Come on, Honey, let me help you. I'll get on one side and you can make the other side."

I quickly began to straighten the spread on her bed before her discouragement could get the best of her. "I don't expect you or Mark to make your beds as well as Polly or Thea, but you have to try over and over and don't give up. Before you know it, you'll be able to make a perfect bed. See? We did it together."

I patted the pillows one last time, squeezed her slightly sagging shoulders, and assured her it would be easier the next time. As I left her room, I detected a trace of pride in her eyes as she set about carefully placing her collection of stuffed animals on her bed. Never before had she had a room of her own and responsibilities of her own. In that moment I felt secure in our decision to require certain things from even the youngest of the kids.

The foster children that have blessed our home were given the same training we gave our own kids. They were required to keep their rooms clean and pick up their clothes and toys.

Kenny, the small boy we had for holidays and summer vacations, told his case worker he didn't want to go anywhere if he couldn't come to our home. When asked why he felt that way, he replied, "because they treat me like one of their own kids. If I messed up my room, they called me back to clean it. If I needed a paddling, they gave it to me."

Children do want discipline, though they may balk at times. It shows them that you care. I know of one teenager who was having extreme difficulty at home and was removed to a foster home. She said to her case worker, "If my mom only knew how to say "no" to me. She acts as though she just doesn't care what I do."

The two foster children we had were then four and six years old. When they first came to us, they couldn't use a toothbrush, didn't know any table manners, and left their room in complete disorder. I knew we must train them, and so began the hard but rewarding task of teaching them independence and responsibility. I began with little things such as leaving the bathroom as clean as they found it. They were taught to get their bed clothes, towel and cloth, take their own baths and clean the bath when they were through, taking their dirty clothes to the utility room. Their room was a greater challenge. They both had a habit of taking their shoes off and dumping the sand and dirt on the carpet. Well, after cleaning the carpet twice, I decided it was time for a lesson. I told them both that every time they dumped their shoes on the carpet, they would have to get the vacuum out, connect it and clean the carpet with my help. The notion of running the carpet sweeper was thrilling at first, but after about a week it became a real chore, especially when they were missing television. I smile now as I remember them then looking for a trash can when they took off their shoes.

I always took one lesson at a time, being careful not to push too much responsibility at them at once. It is amazing how much a four-year old girl can accomplish if we only give her the chance. Both of our young foster children learned to pick up their toys. If they brought a toy into the den, they each knew they were responsible for taking it back to their room after playtime.

I had a small stool in the bath which they stood on to brush their teeth. They both had a habit of leaving the stool there for someone else to move. I noticed the other kids moving it, and one morning I called the two little ones back and told them both they would have to move the stool so no one would trip. It took about a week of reminding, calling one or both of them back, but it paid off and they remembered. After that, moving the stool was a part of the teeth brushing ritual.

Our little six-year old had a habit of stripping his clothes at night and leaving everything wrong-side out, undershirt inside his outer shirt, shorts inside his jeans. I separated them for awhile, and one morning I called him to the washer and explained how he should fix his clothes for the washer. Stopping this habit right then took a little more work off of my shoulders. And would probably save him from being nagged by his wife about this irritating habit! I did not get instant results. But every night that I found his clothes wrong-side out, I put them aside and called him to the washer to straighten them. It took about three or four weeks but I got results!

Some people think, somehow, that small children need to be waited on. They need to be loved unconditionally, but not waited on and continually served . They need discipline and training along with love. The first week the small ones were with us, they would both charge into a room without knocking. Several times they caught the girls dressing. It took time and patience, but I kept reminding them that a closed door means you had to knock. It was just good manners. Sometimes I had to chastise one of them for forgetting, but after several weeks I noticed that they both began to knock and wait for an invitation to come in. When they left us a year later, both of them could hang up their own clothes, clean their room, lead in grace at mealtime, display excellent manners, and show respect for other people.

Many times it would have been easier for me to do for them rather than teaching them to do for themselves. Though this is not the easy way, it's the best way because it prepared them for life outside the security of our home and helped equip them for marriage and families of their own.

Basics of Cooking

I believe that every boy should be able to take over the basics of cooking, so our boys were taught how to prepare a breakfast, cut up a chicken, make tea, start vegetables for dinner, etc. Eddie had been cooking for some time, and Lin was adept at meat cutting, so the job was made easier. Mark, when he was about twelve, could prepare bacon and fry an egg for breakfast and had watched me in the kitchen on numerous occasions. They have also taken their turn washing dishes.

The girls learned quickly that I expected all of them to learn to cook. Every woman can't be an exceptional cook, but every woman can learn how to cook, an essential quality for a wife and mother. As the girls matured and accepted their duties in the kitchen, I was careful to require that they accomplish unfamiliar tasks. In doing so, they learned how to prepare a variety of meals and dishes. Cindy liked to make biscuits, so I made a point to require that the other girls learn how to make them as well. Polly, I discovered one Saturday, didn't know how to make a macaroni and cheese casserole. I promptly turned Sunday's macaroni pie over to her. And the finished product was delicious! One day I asked Janet, our last daughter at home, to cook some rice. I quickly realized that she didn't know how to operate the stove with ease. After several lessons in the kitchen, she quickly learned and mastered the art of cooking.

Since that day, Janet learned to bake cookies, cupcakes, how to prepare bacon and eggs, hamburgers, make tea, and observed me when I required it. I encouraged all the girls to practice in the kitchen, and we ate whatever they made. I still remember Janet's first attempt at cookies when she was eleven. It was a no-bake recipe she had gotten in 4-H class at school. I turned the kitchen over to her one night, explaining the meaning of terms she didn't understand such as "cream butter and sugar", but careful to stay in the den out of her way. The results of her labors were proudly brought to her daddy and me in the den. I have to admit, in all honesty, that those were the oddest oatmeal cookies I'd ever seen or tasted, but the family suffered together as we all exclaimed over the tastiness of her newly acquired recipe. The first few times the girls fried chicken, they seemed to either burn it to a crisp or leave it partly cooked with the juices running. Several times I've seen their dad quietly put a piece on the side of his plate, and I encouraged him to have patience with them as they learned – and learn they did!

Each of the girls was instructed in cooking terms that they would read in recipes from then on – the difference between plain and self-rising flour, the meaning of "whip until foamy", cook until soft-ball stage", "cook at moderate heat", etc. Familiarity with cooking wordage would enable them to be more confident cooks in the kitchen. When a girl marries, she has many challenges facing her, one of which is meeting all of the needs of her husband. If she has a good background in preparing food, she begins her new life with much in her favor. I don't adhere to the belief that "the way to a man's heart is through his stomach", but a husband will be extremely proud of his new wife if she can prepare the foods he likes. All of the girls complained on occasion about having to learn the basics of cooking, but I knew they were all proud of themselves, and their dad and I were proud of them for this accomplishment. Thea, the first to establish a home of her own, quickly discovered the value of having knowledge in the kitchen. Her husband would gladly agree.

Schoolwork

The kids' schoolwork was always their own responsibility. I tried to help the younger ones and remained available for special help with things such as tests or exams. English was always my best subject so I helped them in that area. Their dad offered his help with math. The children also helped each other. Their grades were their ticket to special events or privileges. When a child's grades dropped, and we knew it was because of neglect or unconcern, privileges were cut until their grades improved. I questioned this philosophy for awhile, but it paid off. Most of the kids made good grades and took pride in their schoolwork.

Television

Television became a source of friction in our new home. I really began to notice it soon after Linnie and I were married when I announced no Saturday television until all chores were done. The children seemed to be drawn to the television screen and would even argue over what to watch. Sometimes if we were entertaining friends in the den, I noticed irritation from them because they had to turn the volume down. They began to shut themselves out from activities going on around them, oblivious to others in the den. At times I would call one for a favor or chore, only to be met with a scowl because I took him or her from television.

I also began to notice that the kids would watch anything that was on the screen. If they didn't like one program, they would switch channels and settle on something else. I heard them say several times, "Well, there is nothing else so we'll just watch that" – whether "that" was appropriate or not.

Not being a television fan myself, I wasn't really aware of the type programs the networks were offering. But I began to read everything I could find on the subject in addition to watching television myself for a while. After investigating the children's television habits, I discovered that they were watching all day during summer vacation while Linnie and I were at work. As a result of much research, prayer, and soul searching, Linnie and I came up with some new television restrictions which were received grudgingly at first. During school the television was off limits until 5:00 p.m. After our evening meal no one turned the television on until Linnie or I checked the program listing in the newspaper for informative and interesting programs. If anyone had a specific request, we read the synopsis and watched the program with them. If it proved objectionable, as was the case many times, we requested them to select something of more value. During summer vacation they had certain hours they could watch and they chose the hours they preferred – one hour in the morning, and from 4:00 – 5:30 p.m.in the afternoons. Night viewing remained the same.

There were gripes and frowns at first, but as their interests began to widen, they didn't seem to mind too much. Some of them began to play ball outside, and some would get up a game of croquet. Many afternoons Linnie and I would enter into a game of ball or croquet with them.

Children today are becoming detached from reality. With the influx of technology they are entertained twenty-four hours a day, seven days a week. Most kids today have a smart phone before they are ten years old. Many parents begin allowing their kids to play on these devices before they are one year old. We didn't have a problem with that when we raised our children, but if we had, I am sure we would have set a standard for how long they were on the internet. Parents need to take a strong stand on this issue because already I can see children lacking in verbal skills. They are corresponding so much by texting that they can't converse with each other verbally. Adults are contributing to the problem by being so detached themselves. When Linnie and I go to a restaurant for a meal, 75% of the people there are on these devices, not talking to each other.

Hobbies

As television became part-time entertainment, I noticed the children invading our library of books we kept on hand. I have always loved to work with my hands, sewing, crocheting, and embroidering. I made an afghan for our den and had just begun another one when several of the girls asked about learning. Well, that was encouragement enough for me to invest in yarn for each of the four older girls, and we set about learning to crochet the ripple stitch for an afghan. Janet was only 10 at the time and I knew she was too young for such a large project. So, I got her some rug yarn, and a large needle and showed her a simple stitch which she did not have to count and away she went, exuberant that she was making something!

I kept up with their progress individually, for I knew they may become discouraged and want to quit. Many times I saw one or more of them beginning to rip in disdain, having miscounted the stitches. Julie and Cindy had to be encouraged not to give up because they were younger and were more easily tempted to go to something else. But I never let one of the kids leave a job half-done. I always required that they stick to it until it was finished before starting another project. I don't remember how long it took for all four girls to finish – but they were all proud of their labors and tucked their work in their hope chests for the future. As for Janet – well – she had to be encouraged some too, but she didn't give up. And even if one end of the rug was wider than the other end – she was still proud. And so were we! When Janet started her first afghan, she was fourteen, and very hesitant when I mentioned that it was time to learn. But after I sent her to the store with Julie and Cindy to choose her colors, she returned home proudly carrying her bag filled with yarn and a needle, ready to begin.

For Christmas I always included some type of handwork under the tree. One Christmas I gave the older girls pillow cases to embroider. None of them had done this, but we had fun learning and these, too, were put carefully away for safe-keeping. One year I included pictures in cross-stitch which they hung in their rooms. They also became interested in crewel and we invested in crewel pillows for each of them. It took Janet a little longer to master new projects, being three years younger, but she quickly caught up. Janet got her own crewel beginner kit for Christmas one year which she quickly completed. I never considered buying these materials a waste, but rather an investment. These special abilities have accompanied these girls into their adult lives and I am hopeful they will pass them on to their own children.

Decisions, Decisions

Making decisions was another area of training for our children. They were all taught that each person must begin to make decisions at an early age, beginning with small decisions like what to wear. This developed into more complex ones such as selecting friends and selecting a career. There is a point in every child's life when he must take responsibility for his actions. Our kids were taught that they should weigh each decision carefully in light of circumstances because they were responsible for every decision they made. It is important not to push too many decisions on a child too soon, but if he is allowed to make minor ones at an early age, it will be easier for him to develop good decision-making habits in the teen years when the decisions begin to shape his life.

If one of the kids came to Linnie and me about a decision, we always tried to be open to both sides of the issue, state any objections we may have and the reason for the objection, and ask the child to think it through and to pray about it. This practice never failed and in most cases the young people in our home made wise decisions. They knew that whatever decision was made, they were responsible for the consequences.

We had one particular experience in which we thought a very foolish decision had been made, but as it worked out the decision proved to be a well learned lesson for several people. Lin was in college and was driving a rather old car. He came to us one day in October with the proposal of making a trip to the mountains of North Carolina one weekend with his sister, Polly, a student nurse, and another student nurse he had been dating. Linnie and I both gave Lin our opinion, stating that we did not think the car could stand a trip like that. We cautioned him about the risks involved concerning the insurance coverage and the possibility of a law suit if an accident should occur. His desire to show these girls a good time won out over his sound judgement, and on Friday morning he pulled out of the yard at 7:00 a.m.in sub-freezing temperatures to pick up the girls at their dorm. I prayed for him, feeling that he had made a poor decision. On Sunday morning at 8:30 a.m., as we were hurriedly dressing for church, the phone rang. Somehow I knew it was Lin. His voice was tense. "Daddy, I've got a problem. The clutch on the car gave out last night on the top of Mt. Pisgah, North Carolina. A nice couple gave us a ride back to Clemson where we spent the night. The girls are fine but they have to be back at the dorm by 9:00 p.m. tonight. Could you come and get us?"

I prayed a silent prayer of thanksgiving, feeling that God had truly protected them and would make good out of the situation. However, Linnie did not share my enthusiasm as he "lost his cool" after telling Lin we would come and get them. I didn't want Linnie to make the trip alone so I quickly called the kids together, told them of the situation, and that I would accompany their dad to North Carolina to bring everyone home-the kids and the car.

Thea was still at home so she took charge of getting the kids to church and getting dinner. By 9:30 a.m. we were on the road, Linnie still raving about kids making foolish decisions and how he was going to really "tell Lin how he felt" when we got to Clemson.

I am still thankful that it took three hours to get to the campus because it took me all of those precious hours to calm Linnie and convince him that no chastisement from us would be necessary in this case. I explained for a long time, "Lin is embarrassed and humiliated over this situation, Linnie. I think he knows that he made a poor decision without our telling him. I know how much he must have hated calling home for help. But he _did_ make that call, and we are going to help. I feel that Lin has learned a valuable lesson and any further humiliation is unnecessary, Babe. Please don't embarrass him in the presence of his girl." I went on and on pleading with Linnie to accept this situation and try to make some good come out of it.

By the time we located the dorm where the girls were staying, Linnie had calmed down quite a bit. There were three sad, dejected young people who got into our car very quietly that day. No one said a word, but a tenseness permeated the car. As we began the drive to pick up the car, I tried to make casual conversation but finally gave up, and we drove on in silence. We finally got something to eat around 3:30 p.m. which helped a little. The farther we got into the mountains, the foggier and colder it became. By the time we reached the parking lot at the summit of Mt. Pisgah at 5:00 p.m., visibility was near 0, with a temperature of 32 degrees with winds around 30 mph, causing the chill factor to be considerably lower. Linnie's "chill factor" was equally low.

This is going to be hard for some to believe (except those of us who were there) but as we drove into the parking lot to hook up the tow-bar and bring the car home, the brakes failed on our car! I did not know how much more Linnie could take and still control himself, but I kept saying "There's no need to get excited – just be patient." I didn't think my words were helping much as he and Lin got out and tried to operate Lin's car, to no avail. We girls sat in the car and watched as icicles formed on the trees nearby while the temperature dropped rapidly.

We left Lin's car in the care of the park ranger, drove down the mountain at 10 mph with the help of the emergency brake and located a wrecker service which agreed to go up on Monday, pull the car down and repair it (another miracle of our great God). We called the dorm to let the supervisor know the girls would be late, called home to ease the other children's minds, and left Asheville for the long, slow drive home. Thank goodness the entire trip home was on Interstate 26 which made driving, with very little brakes, easier. I drove most of the way home, insisting that Linnie get some rest. We reached home at 10:35 p.m., and I can truthfully say home never looked so beautiful.

The kids were still up waiting with hot supper ready for us. All I wanted was a hot bath and a bed, but I managed to eat a little. I know of five very tired people who had no trouble sleeping that night!

Lin never mentioned the incident again and neither did we. None of us had to. I've always hated the words "I told you so". Sometimes the "unspoken" lessons are the most valuable. Lin was aware, I am sure, of his dad's struggle not to lose his temper. And I was extremely proud of Linnie because I was also aware of his struggle. The weekend cost Lin over $150 in repair and tow bills in addition to the bruises to his male ego. I seriously doubted if he would ever attempt such an excursion again. And Linnie and I learned another lesson in patience. The cost to us? A little frustration, a little inconvenience, an unplanned trip. Such is the price of parenthood!

I tried not to give our children specific commands unless I was pressed for time and had to meet a deadline. If there were several special jobs which needed to be done, I called them together and said "Look, we've got some work to do. You can pick which jobs you each want. We have until 5:00 p.m.to finish." This gave them an opportunity to choose which job they preferred. They also got to choose when to do their regular chores within certain limits. Janet, who was now folding clothes, could fold when she liked – but – they had to be folded and delivered by the time I arrived at home from work. Most of the kids have told me on occasions that they were glad we required them to accept responsibility. And that they had choices about when to complete given tasks.

If more parents would require, no, demand that their children be responsible for certain chores, we would see more young adults entering the workforce with a strong work ethic, committed to hard work, and a tenacity in their chosen field. So many parents are often guilty of wanting their children to have the comforts of life that they were deprived of and tend to smother their children with material things, never requiring them to have jobs or accept any responsibility.

All of our children knew what it meant to save allowance for a movie or a skating party, to first give their tithe to God, or to do without an extra pair of shoes so a brother or sister could have a pair. I was tempted at times to be guilty of indulgence with the children, but then I realized the tremendous values they were learning.

Several times each year we had a special offering for missions in our church. At our home we always put the envelope on the dining table and asked each member of the family to drop in anything they wished to give. It became a joint venture for all of us trying to reach a goal we had set as a family. We were closing an offering on one occasion when Janet said, "Wait, I forgot to put in my share." On another occasion all the kids wanted to go bowling with the church youth group and Mark informed us that he wasn't going. When asked why, he replied, "I spent some of my allowance on something for myself. If I go bowling, there won't be enough left for God on Sunday." Mark made a decision, and he stuck with it. He stayed home from that bowling trip. I silently offered a prayer of gratitude to God that we were blessed with such wonderful children. In his decision to stay at home that night, Mark learned a great lesson in giving.

Moments like these illustrate their unselfishness and concern for others which they had learned. We have tried to teach them that it is truly "more blessed to give than to receive" and I believe that all of our kids have felt the joy that comes from giving to God and others.

My pride in our children is evident, and they are all exceptional people. The truth that you always receive more than you give has been proven in our home through the years. Our eight kids gave up a great deal in order to make our new home function in peace and harmony. And we have all gained so much in unselfishness and love.

It is a great privilege bring a parent – and also a great responsibility and challenge. God placed these lives with us and expects us to "train them up in the way they should go." The great task of parenthood weighed very heavily on me at times during the first challenging year, especially when a crisis arose. With each decision I prayed that God would guide both Linnie and me, giving us both discernment and wisdom so that all of us could pull together as a team.

God's Time

Another vital part of our children's training was their religious heritage. Someone said to me once, "I don't believe in making children to go church. This should be a personal decision." We didn't assume this philosophy with our children. We sent our kids to school – made them go – in order for them to be equipped for life. It was just as important for our children to be schooled in God's Word and His will. This was never a choice. As mandated in Deuteronomy 11:18-19, *"Fix these words of mine in your hearts and minds; tie them as symbols on your hands and bind them on your foreheads. Teach them to your children, talking about them when you sit at home and when you walk along the road, when you lie down and when you get up."* It is a tremendous responsibility to lead a child from birth to an acute awareness of the presence of Christ, and to continue their religious education as long as they are in our care. We always required the young people in our home to attend church and encouraged them to be active in the church's activities. If one of our kids went off for a weekend, we always asked that they find a church to attend on Sunday. We always tried to "live" our faith and not just "preach" it and this makes the difference. We were active in our church and, as a result, so were the kids. Most of them were in the youth choir, one of our teenagers taught a Sunday school class, and one year two of our girls helped with vacation Bible school. We had nightly devotion time in our home which proved to be a marvelous experience for all of us.

Each child in our family was encouraged to have his own "time alone with God" to tell God about personal needs and to pray for others. If any one of them was having a problem, we encouraged him to pray about it, asking for God's guidance. In addition to family prayer, Linnie and I had our own quiet time and prayed together for our family. All of our children made the decision to accept Christ into their hearts, and this is the greatest joy a parent can experience. One evening I heard a knock on my bathroom door. There stood Mark and Janet, our two youngest children. Excitedly, they said, "Mom, we want to ask Jesus to be our Savior. And we want to be baptized." I was never so thrilled to hear knocks on my bathroom door that night! It was one of the most beautiful memories I stored away in my heart. I believe the multitude of blessings God has given us through the years is a result of doing everything, including the training of His children, according to His instructions.

As the kids grew up and "left the nest", they have made independent choices. With adulthood comes the assurance that all choices result in consequences- good and bad. It is my prayer that every one of the children seek God daily, to put Him first in their lives, and rest on the truths learned while at home. I find peace in God's promise, *"Bring up a child in the way he should go, and when he is old, he will not depart from it."* (Proverbs 22:6)

Training a child is never an easy task for a parent, and it has not been easy for Linnie and me. In carrying out our sacred and honored task, we've made many mistakes, blundered through hasty decisions, and at times still wonder if some of our labors were in vain. Our eight wonderful children have made an "impossible" job not only "possible" but beautiful as well, because of their understanding and love. Even though they didn't understand and agree with some of our decisions at times, they always seemed to know that we were doing the best that we could, and that we made mistakes and blunders too. Above all they knew we loved them and always would. *"For whom the Lord loves he corrects, even as a father corrects the son in whom he delights."* (Proverbs 3:11-12)

Chapter 18

CONQUERING GOLIATH

"Annette, I am detecting a thickness in your left breast," Dr. Lawton Salley said. " I don't mean to alarm you, but I feel that you should contact a breast surgeon as soon as possible to determine what's going on. Do you have a preference of who you'd like to see?"

My heart began to pound in my chest. "Oh, God, what does this mean? Do I have cancer? I don't have time to have cancer! I'm in the prime of my life. Take this away from me, dear Jesus! I don't even know a surgeon. I need your wisdom and your peace."

Dr. Salley was waiting on my reply, so I focused to answer his question. "I don't know a surgeon, but I'm sure I want to go to Columbia for an appointment. My daughter-in-law is related to Dr. Charles Harmon of Lexington. I could go to him."

"I will get my nurse to make the appointment for you. Let's get a mammogram done as soon as possible so you can carry that with you."

He left the room and I was left with my thoughts in a jumble. "I can't do this, Lord. Why, me? Haven't I been through enough rough times in my life? I want to see my grandchildren grow up!"

My thoughts were interrupted by Dr. Salley's return. "I made you an appointment with Dr. Harmon for next Monday. I don't want to put this off. I also have an appointment for a mammogram which you can have done in Orangeburg."

I left his office in a blur and rode home with more questions invading my thoughts. What did this mean? What if they had to remove my breast? How would I look? Would I still be desirable to Linnie? What if it meant that both breasts had to come off? Would I feel like a whole woman? Ever? How would I break this bad news to Linnie? I prayed and cried the whole drive home.

While we had supper that night, Linnie gave me a hard look and asked, "Squirt, you look like you have something on your mind. Is something up with the kids? Is it the appointment with the doctor today?

I broke the news to Linnie and held my breath when I finished telling about my appointment in Lexington with Dr. Charles Harmon. Linnie took my hand and said, "You know I love you more than life, right? I would love you just as much if you had one arm or one leg. We will go through this trial together, you and me and Jesus.

I fell into his arms, and the dam of tears suddenly broke. He held me until I was spent, and I felt complete peace. I should have known he would understand and react as he had. This problem couldn't be as bad as I thought. It may be a simple cyst that Dr. Harmon has to remove and then we will get back to living again. "Thank you, Lord, for Your peace. Continue to show me Your will for my life in the midst of uncertainty." "Let's not share this news with the kids yet until we know something concrete to tell them."

Monday came much too soon, and we were sitting in Dr. Harmon's office. Linnie had taken the day off to go with me to the surgeon's office. The doctor took a long time viewing the mammogram, and then entered the exam room.

"Mrs. Sutcliffe, I have taken a good look at the film. The only way to really be able to tell what we're dealing with is to do a biopsy. If it is agreeable with both of you, I will set up the surgery with Lexington Medical Center. It is done as a one-day surgery, so you will be able to go home that afternoon. It should be done as soon as possible."

He set up the surgical appointment and assured us that it could be a simple cyst that needed to be removed. We left his office and began the trip home. "Oh, Babe, I'm frightened! Everything is happening so quickly, I can't absorb it all. Do you think this is something simple?"

"Squirt, do you remember I told you not to worry so much about the unknown? I think we have a good, Christian surgeon, and we need to put ourselves in his hands because I believe he puts himself in God's hands."

"Linnie, thank you for your wisdom. I've always been a worrier at heart. I don't know what I'd do without you. Thank you for loving me through this."

The biopsy was performed, and Dr. Harmon breezed into the room with the announcement. "Mrs. Annette, it was a benign cyst! You are going to be back to normal living in just a few days."

"Oh, thank you Dr. Harmon! Thank you for the gift of life!" He shook his head and replied, "Oh, you need to thank the Lord, this is His doing. I was only his instrument. I would like a follow-up mammogram though. You can have it done in Orangeburg or in Columbia."

I was so excited, I talked the whole way back home. "Now, we can tell the kids that it was nothing to be dreading or to be worried about. Let's celebrate! Go out to supper."

"Okay", Linnie laughed. "I don't believe you were this excited when we got married."

The follow-up mammogram was made and sent to Dr. Harmon's office. The following week, we found ourselves back in his exam room. He entered and got right down to business. "Mrs. Annette, the mammogram you just had done shows a mass deeply embedded under where the cyst was. I am so sorry. We need to do immediate surgery, and if it is cancer, we need to either do a lumpectomy or a radical mastectomy. Something told me to do a follow-up mammogram because the "thickness" to the touch indicated cancer." He went on to describe the difference between a lumpectomy and a mastectomy, but I was numb with fear and trepidation of the unknown, and I only heard half of what he said. He said he would take some lymph nodes from under the left arm and if they showed that the cancer had filtered through them into the rest of my body, I would have to go through six months of chemotherapy.

"Dr. Harmon, I believe I want that breast off and gone from my body. I don't want to take the chance that even a tiny part of the cancer remains after a lumpectomy. Make the arrangements at the medical center as soon as possible, and let's get it done."

All of the children were upset with the news that I had breast cancer, and Linnie and I played it down as best we could. The surgery was performed on October 13, 1989, three days after we found out about the cancer, and the wait began again to find out about the lymph nodes. Two days later an oncologist walked into my hospital room and said, "Mrs. Sutcliffe, some of your lymph nodes were positive, so we have to be looking at some chemotherapy. Did Dr. Harmon advise you of the possibility of chemo?"

I could hardly answer in the affirmative, I was so shocked to hear this news. I really thought I had reached a plateau in my faith where worry was not taking over in my mind and heart. But this news was not good at all! The oncologist continued going over the regimen that I would be living with for six months and left me with a cornucopia of booklets on going through chemo. About that time Linnie came in, and I shared the information with him. "Babe", I am determined to lick this disease called "cancer". You're going to have to walk beside me, you and Jesus, to get it done.

"We'll get it done together, "Squirt", the two of us, and Jesus. And I'll bet you will be able to help other women who are walking this road after you."

I decided that my mom would drive me to my first chemo treatment since Linnie had to work. I took a tape player with earphones with me and listened to praise music the entire time the needle was flooding my body with chemotherapy. It went without incident, and Mom and I stopped at Shoney's for some soup and water. "Do you feel okay?" she asked. "I feel just fine. I am not sick at all." We stopped at the drug store on the way home to get my prescriptions filled for nausea meds and also the oral chemo which the oncologist had given me.

I took all of my medications that night and still felt fine. I have had insomnia all of my life, and it took me a long time to get to sleep. Linnie held me and told me he loved me, and I finally drifted off to sleep.

At about 5:00 a.m., it began. Powerful waves of nausea invaded my body, and I began to throw up. People from our church were beginning to stop by and bring me food, but I could hardly talk to them I was so violently sick. Time after time all day I was in the bathroom, leaning over my toilet. This went on for three days until finally I called Dr. Jones, my oncologist. The nurse called me back and asked, "Mrs. Sutcliffe, when are you taking your oral chemo, Cytoxan?" "I'm taking it with my other meds, at night." "Oh, no, never take it at night. Take it in the morning after your breakfast, and I believe you will be able to tolerate it. If you take it at night, the medication just sits there in your system, and causes extreme nausea the following morning."

I felt as if she had given me a precious gift! I began to take the med after my breakfast, and the results were much better. I was still a little sick to my stomach but the nausea meds helped with that.

I had some normal fears when I began my journey without my breast and one of them was facing Linnie when I undressed for the first time. I postponed facing him for a week or two but knew there had to be a first time. So, one night as I donned my nightgown, I turned to face him, and he looked at me and said, "You are so beautiful." He gave me another reason by that statement to beat this horrible disease.

My sister from Delaware was visiting my mom for a week, and they took me for my appointment to be fitted for a breast prosthesis. We stopped on the way and had a nice salad for lunch.

In the middle of my appointment I began to feel sick but managed to get through and purchased some bras and a prosthesis. As we began our trip home, I felt really bad and asked them to stop at a fast-food restaurant. We stopped at Hardees, and I threw up my lunch in their restroom. So much for a nice trip.

After my second chemo treatment, I was taking my shower one night when I noticed large chunks of hair in my hands. I knew it was going to happen, but I wasn't ready for it. "Oh, God, not this, too! I can't take any more, Father! Please remove this. Don't take my hair, too. I need your grace to handle what I must!" Losing my hair was almost as traumatic for me as losing my breast. I can't speak for other women, but this was a milestone I didn't think I could endure. I yelled for Linnie and he comforted me as best he could. "Sweetheart, we knew this was likely a result of your treatment. We will weather it just like all the other things you are going through. You are beautiful to me, whatever you may look like. I am off tomorrow and we can look for a wig for you to wear when you go out."

The next day we shopped and found a wig, one that closely resembled my own hair. I had recently gone back to work at the plant on a part-time basis and wore the wig for the first time. Everyone there was extremely supportive and kept telling me how good I looked, even though I thought they were just being nice.

Several days later I was at work one day when I began to feel really bad, and quickly had a chill. I was sure that I was taking the flu, so I left work, went home, and got in bed. I had aching bones and couldn't get warm. Supper went undone and Linnie found me in bed when he got home from work. He said, "Don't worry about supper, I'll get something started and also prepare some soup for you. Does your throat hurt? Are you congested?" he asked. "No, I'm just sore all over and can't get warm. It must be the beginning of the flu."

The next morning I felt just fine and got up and ate a good breakfast. "I don't know what happened, but now I feel just fine. I'm going to work."

That night I read over the side effects of having chemo, and there it was. Many times it would cause flu-like symptoms, especially after having a recent treatment. Now it was evident to me what was going on! That awful chemo which was attacking my infected, cancerous cells and killing them, was also attacking my good cells at the same time, making me sick! Several more times during the course of my six-month treatments, I would have to leave work because of feeling so badly.

My oncologist told me that I needed to ingest more calories because I had lost so much weight. Nothing tasted good to me because I had that constant nausea that goes along with chemo. It was the first and only time in my life that I tried to gain weight. Linnie would make chocolate milkshakes at night and we would both drink them. He was the one that was gaining weight instead of me so we ended up having to cut back!

One morning I woke up early and noticed that my mouth was very sore. By the time I went to work I was covered on the inside of my mouth with sores. I could only ingest soup or something very soft. Dr. Jones was called and he called in a mouthwash called "Miracle Mouthwash" which helped some. But after the next treatment, the same thing happened. I then began to notice that my nostrils were also infected with the sores which sometimes bled. My nose stayed stopped up for weeks at a time.

My brothers and sisters in our church were extremely good to me during that time in my life and continued to bring food to us. Every time I was a little down in the dumps, I would get an encouraging card or call. I kept my cards for several years and would often read them over and over again.

One day when I was alone at home, I was sitting out on our porch reading my Bible and talking to the Lord. I suddenly began to sob, tears coursing down my cheeks and I was crying out again to God. "God in heaven, I am not sure I can finish this treatment. You are going to have to hold me up or I'll just fall apart!" Just about that time, the phone rang. It was one of the girls from work. "I just felt like calling and telling you we miss you," she said. We talked for a few minutes, she prayed for me, and I felt so much better when the conversation ended. "Thanks Lord, for visiting me today," I said, smiling to myself. "You always surpass my expectations! Thank You for being such a great God!" That's just a sample of the support and encouragement that I received during that bad time in my life.

Time marched on and the weeks turned into months and the six months was almost over for me. I began to think, "What now? What's next for me in my life?" My hair was beginning to peek through the skin, and I was elated at getting hair again! I remembered a few of my "bad days" when I wondered, "What if I never get my hair back? What will I do?" I'll never forget the first time I went to my hairdresser to have my little wisps of hair done. I told her, "You are a miracle worker, you know that?" when she finished. It actually looked pretty good, and everyone at work remarked on how great I looked with hair!

I was having my quiet time one morning and I came across the scripture in 2 Corinthians 1:3b-4. *"Blessed be the Father of mercies and the God of all comfort who comforts us in all of our affliction so that we may be able to comfort those who are in any affliction with the comfort with which we ourselves are comforted by God."* It jumped out at me and I finally understood what God was trying to tell me. It was like He was saying, "See, Annette, this is what I expect of you, to share with others who are facing what you just faced and won the victory. Go out, my daughter, and minister to others."

And thus began my encouragement ministry which I am still engaged in, some thirty years later. When I become aware of a woman who has breast cancer and is just beginning her journey, I try to call her if possible, send cards periodically, and covenant to pray for her daily. I heard through a friend of a program called "Reach to Recovery", and I became involved in that ministry for about eight years until it was discontinued. I have ministered to over 150 women in this way.

On the last day of chemo, Linnie took the day off and went

with me for the treatment. We were going to celebrate the victory together by going out to lunch. Well, by the time the treatment was over, I was so sick we had to go straight home! I was so disappointed I almost cried in the car, but I was too happy to be sad! It was over! My days would begin to get better now, and I would soon be back to normal. "Oh, thank you, Jesus, for walking with me through this journey. Thank You for some good days, and even for the really bad days, for You were constantly holding me up, and we weathered the storm together. And thank you, Linnie, for being with me and sometimes carrying me yourself during the many stressful days."

Young Annette

Young Linnie

The children making a pyramid

Julie blowing out her birthday candles

Honey harvest time

Annette and Linnie clowing around

Enjoying retirement

Annette and Linnie in New York for the National
Mother of the Year competition

Surrounded by the children at the S.C.
Mother of the Year press conference

Celebrating Linnie's 80th birthday

The children at Linnie's 80th birthday party

PART 2

Chapter 19

REFLECTIONS

You have been reading many of my reflections from our family of ten and how we managed to stay together for forty-six years. The Holy Spirit guided our family during the good times as well as some very hard experiences and many seasons of testing. This story has been my voice. However, I think it only fair to hear from some of the children in our household of faith. So, enjoy their voices as well.

Polly

I am Polly, the middle of Dad's five children, which consists of four girls and one boy. I was twelve when we all weathered a rather rough storm with Dad. Divorce. Without Dad's strength and steadfast determination to keep his children together, we would have been divided for a time. But, thankfully, he persevered and we all stayed with him.

My memories of events over the following few years are vague. I'm sure we settled into a routine of housekeeping and schooling . . . and probably gardening too, for I can't imagine us not having a garden . . . ever. On weekends we girls did the laundry and cleaned house. Dad has always been a good cook, and with the occasional contribution of soup from Grandma Sutcliffe, we survived.

However, I do remember clearly how I felt. Most importantly, I felt safe residing in my father's home with my siblings. But beneath that blanket of security loomed confusion and disorientation, as I am sure is the case for many children following the divorce of their parents. One often hears people comment on how resilient children are, how they are so capable of rebounding after difficulties such as divorce. While I agree that they are adaptable, to a point, I doubt that many adults pause to acknowledge to what degree children are permanently changed by such devastating events. I, for one, couldn't imagine my future beyond the following month, had no hope for what life might hold for me beyond the boundaries of Norway and certainly had no aspirations to conquer the world. I lacked confidence and a sense of direction. Then . . . Mom showed up.

"Momma-nette", as we initially called her when she and dad were dating, very soon became just "Momma", and her three children became our brothers and sister, not step-brothers and step-sister. (The "S" word is reserved for use only in explaining to strangers the anomaly formed by our family.) Momma brought organization to our lives on many levels as she partnered with Dad to raise eight very individual children. I remember her leaving instructions regarding household routines posted in conspicuous places signed "The Management." As a team, she and Dad also helped each child to identify their strengths and gave sound counsel on possible life vocations. It is because of their efforts to establish a disciplined, organized and Christ-centered household that I gradually came to feel as if I was a valued member of a unified successful team.

The following are some of my favorite memories of us all working together to accomplish a given task.

Daily, Mom left a menu for that evening's supper posted on the refrigerator door. At about 4:00 p.m., we girls would meet in the kitchen and each pick an item we were willing to cook. By the time Mom and Dad arrived from work, we had the meal cooked, the table set, and we all gathered to eat. Afterwards our parents would retire to the den and we girls cleaned and put away the dishes. If ever Mom was asked how she survived without a dishwasher, she simply replied, "I have five of them."

Then there was grocery day. Mom and Dad would go every two weeks to the grocery store, without any children! They would each fill a buggy. When they drove into the yard we children would form a line from the car to the house to get the groceries inside. A few would get the large packages of meat and divide them as instructed, wrap the portions in freezer paper, label them and load them into the inside or outside freezers. Others would tackle items that needed to go into the pantry or the fridge, and then others would grab the things that went into the large bathroom closet. The two youngest children stationed themselves beneath the large kitchen table to receive the emptied paper bags which they would promptly fold and stack. In no time at all we had everything put away and everything tidy again.

I also remember Lin coming home from Clemson University for Christmas break and all of us going with him to cut trees for firewood. As he used the chainsaw to cut and strip the tree, the rest of us would move in close and pull away all the smaller limbs and keep everything organized. We girls would work together to get the logs onto the truck, and before long we would have a load. On one occasion, Cindy was standing on top of a tree trunk blaring out a song as loud as she could. She felt confident because nobody could hear a note over the loud buzzing of the saw. It was quite humorous when Lin suddenly turned it off!

Baling hay was an adventure as well. Dad would drive the tractor with the baler attached and Mark, I'm sure barely able to reach the gas or brake, would ease the pickup truck along. Some of us would throw the bales into the back of the truck while others would be there to stack it. Cindy and I would work together, one on each end of a bale. Julie was always taller and stronger, for she takes after the Young side of the family, and could manage one all on her own.

What I remember most clearly is the big grin on Mark's face. He definitely had the best job!

Many hands do make light work. To this day, if I am overwhelmed when working to complete a complicated task, I look back and remember those times with fondness. I imagine my siblings working alongside me, and it helps me get the job done.

Mt. Pisgah

While I was a nursing student in Orangeburg and my brother, Lin, was at Clemson University, he began dating one of my classmates. Lin asked to take us to the Blue Ridge Parkway one weekend. He picked us up from our dorm on Saturday morning with plans to explore the parkway that afternoon, stay at Clemson that night and return to Orangeburg before our dorm's nine o'clock curfew Sunday evening. I didn't mind being the third wheel and, as a sleep-deprived student, was determined to curl up in the back seat with a blanket and pillow and snooze as much as possible!

I settled in quickly for the long, four-hour trip and was drifting in and out of sleep as we cruised the parkway in Lin's Pinto, a small circa 1970's economy car. It was somewhere on Mt. Pisgah that Lin began his epic battle with the vehicle's manual transmission! He had always lifted weights and kept a decent set of biceps, so was well prepared for combat. I remember being awakened by a grinding sound and finally forced myself to open my eyes, still in a fog, to the sight of Lin holding the stick shift in his hand . . . I mean free from the transmission . . . in his hand! I just stared for a moment, unable to comprehend the strange sight. It didn't take long for reality to set in and the reality was: we were on Mt. Pisgah, weather had moved in and it was cold, wet and foggy, we had no stick shift and, worst of all, we were going to have to call Dad for help!

A quick side note. Anytime Daddy is referenced in these writings, just think . . . John Wayne. Daddy reminds me of him in many ways. He is built like the actor, standing at a good height, with a broad chest and square hips. Daddy also shares the attitudes of many of the characters John Wayne portrayed in that here is a man who holds deep convictions in regards to God, country and family. He will help anyone who will try to help themselves but will hold accountable those who mess up. He has no patience with bad manners and should you choose to be disrespectful to him in his house, you should do so with one foot out the door . . . to give yourself a head start.

Back to the story. As God would have it, a couple from Clemson were driving behind us on the mountain. The man had brought his wife for a scenic drive for her birthday during which he realized Lin was having difficulties. Thankfully, they were kind enough to give us a lift to Clemson. (A God thing!)

After seeing that my classmate and I were settled in for the night, Lin retreated to his dorm room to start making calls. He stayed up late trying to find someone who could help get us back to Orangeburg by curfew on Sunday. He desperately wanted to avoid calling home because Dad and Mom had both strongly cautioned Lin not to take the Pinto into the mountains. I'm sure it was with great reluctance and dread that he called our parents early the next morning . . . John Wayne it would be.

As we waited nervously for Mom and Dad's arrival, I began to formulate a plan in which I could remove myself from the situation as much as possible. When they arrived I would simply crawl into the very back of the station wagon, blanket and pillow in tow, to hibernate until we reached Orangeburg, which was an hour beyond Columbia. Surely Dad could make arrangements for Lin's car with a few phone calls, and we would be on our way. Imagine my despair when the Maverick, another small circa 1970's economy car, rounded the corner instead of the large comfortable family wagon I had counted on. And then more despair when Dad announced that we were heading back to Pisgah, in the opposite direction from home, to find the Pinto and talk to a local garage! Scotty, beam me up! (That would be the first of three such requests to Scotty during this trip.)

We all settled into the Maverick for the two-hour trek back to the mountains. I sat in the back behind Dad. Lin valiantly sat in the middle, on the hump, with his date to his right. The drive back to Mt. Pisgah was quiet despite the tense atmosphere. I imagined that Mom had encouraged Dad, during the long drive to Clemson, to try to remain calm. The weather on the mountain had persisted. It continued to be foggy, wet, and very cold, resulting in the overnight formation of icicles on the evergreens. Visibility was poor and Daddy was having to go in and out of each parking lot to locate the abandoned car before we finally spotted it. As he drew closer to Lin's car to come to a stop, it happened . . . the brakes on the Maverick failed. Dad skillfully used the emergency brake to bring the car safely to a stop.

I could feel the rumble of emotion building in Dad as he sprang from his seat, threw up the hood and stood on the passenger side, closest to Mom, to examine the engine. (Scotty Request #2) My most vivid memory during this event is of Mom rapidly knocking on the windshield to get Dad's attention and then pointing her finger at him. On that day I witnessed the power of the right index finger of a tiny woman to calm an impending eruption of anger that would have flowed over us all.

After quickly establishing that the Pinto had endured the night on the mountain without being vandalized, we headed back down to find a garage. Dad drove slowly in the wintery environment, engaging the emergency brake when necessary, and arrived safely at a garage. The mechanic agreed to tow Lin's car before dark and to make repairs. We then began the long slow journey home in the crippled Maverick.

Dad had to go cautiously slow, turning a four-hour trip into what felt like eternity. I had long since filled my need for sleep and could slumber no more to escape the ordeal. We had traveled for miles and darkness had come, erasing my ability to establish any bearings. I didn't know how much longer I could stay seated without the ability to stretch and didn't dare ask where we were. I became as restless as a caged cat. At one point I balled up my blanket and put it under me, planted my feet as far under Dad's seat as I dared go and straightened out to place the side of my face against the back windshield to find a few moments of relief.

Shortly afterwards I began looking for a road sign that would give me some indication as to how much longer this journey would last. Finally I could detect an approaching sign and was instantly filled with anticipation. The slower than normal speed of the car delayed my ability to actually read it for several moments. Then slowly but surely, the stark cold truth was revealed, printed on that stoic metal sign standing in the darkness: Columbia 96 mi. (Scotty Request #3)

We would miraculously arrive safely back at the dorm before curfew and life would return back to normal for everyone, after having both cars repaired. However, I would avoid the mountains for nearly twenty years! I had absolutely no interest in traveling to those altitudes and kept strictly to the beach on vacations. Finally, when our children were young, my husband and I began driving to Little Rock, Arkansas, at least every other year, to visit his grandmother. On those journeys through Tennessee I fell in love with the mountains. The hills and valleys, the shadows and coolness, the babbling brooks and thundering falls, the majestic rocky peaks and mighty spruce reaching for the skies. God and peace.

Poison Oak

Bethany Baptist Church is a picturesque white church that sits back off a country road in a grove of tall pines. During my teenage years it had an unusually large number of youth for its small size. There were a handful of adults that were committed to these youths and blessed our lives tremendously. I remember going

Christmas caroling around the countryside in a tractor-pulled trailer, Christmas and Halloween parties, volleyball, basketball, ping pong, and music, music, music.

The girls in our family participated in the Acteens program at Bethany. This was a biblically based program in which teenage girls could advance through different levels by being actively involved in such things as community service projects, missions, Bible study and memorizing scripture. The church would hold an annual recognition service, presenting awards to the girls who had achieved the next level. It was really a big deal!

The participants would wear long dresses and be presented with a crown, scepter or cape, depending on which level each had accomplished. I remember one such ceremony in particular. Following a long year of Wednesday night meetings and projects, the weekend of the awards service had finally arrived. With Mom's help, we had each completed making our dresses and were prepared for the Saturday evening event.

With time to spare, Cindy and I decided to go up to the old home place on Saturday morning to gather some wild strawberry plants. We both loved strawberries and had prepared a place in the sun, behind one of Dad's sheds, where we could pamper these plants and hopefully harvest some of their luscious fruit.

The old home place was Grandma Sutcliffe's family home where my great-grandparents, Luther and Julia Young, raised their large family. It was located behind Grandma's property and within walking distance from our house. The homestead consisted of an old farmhouse surrounded by multiple barns, sheds, a chicken coop and a well. It all sat beneath a canopy of pecan trees on the back side with tall elms on the front and provided a great place to explore, if you dared.

You see, the place was inherited by my great aunt who lived away. She had locked it up, completely furnished, plates in the cupboards, coffee pot on the stove, papers in the desk . . . as tight as a time capsule. With Grandma Sutcliffe's help, we would occasionally "break in" and thumb through old school books and catalogs and rummage through closets as we imagined the lives of our loved ones who had lived there years ago. We would always be sure to leave things just as they were when we left, lest our visit be detected by our formidable great aunt.

That sense of foreboding remained with us that Saturday morning as Cindy and I stepped from my grandmother's yard and into the grove of pecan trees that separated the two properties. While digging the ground beneath the pecan trees, we were careful to stay away from some poison oak rambling nearby. We were confident we had avoided it as we walked home to put our little prizes to bed. We watered and fertilized the plants and imagined the fresh fruit and jam we would enjoy as a result of all our efforts.

That evening after supper, we hurried to get dressed for our ceremony. Teenage girls always want to look their very best for such events and we were no exception. Dresses, hair, makeup and nails all had to be perfect if we were going to be paraded in front of the rest of the church members. As the evening progressed, Cindy and I started itching a little. Cindy could tell she was going to have a patch on one arm and one side of her face but didn't realize how severe those patches would become. My eyes became reddened and itchy, and I generally just didn't feel well, but we made it through the evening.

I was awakened in the middle of the night with intense itching ALL OVER and was devastated to look into the bathroom mirror to see a slightly swollen face, covered in a horrid red rash. Of course it progressed through Sunday and by Monday morning we were both a mess. Cindy's areas had intensified to the point of misery, and I was covered from head to toe. Every feature on my head was swollen to twice its normal size . . . eyes, nose, lips and ears. (I would see a film about the Elephant Man several years later, and I couldn't help but feel a little kinship to Joseph Merrick.) We looked so diseased that the doctor let us use the back door of his office.

After careful examination and shots, the doctor sent Cindy

and me home with "itch pills" and a school excuse. We took turns lying on the vinyl sofa because it felt cooler to our skin than the other one upholstered in a rough woolen fabric. We were partners in misery as we took the little green pills and slept as much as possible. Because the poison oak had entered my blood stream, I would return to the doctor a few more times for more shots and was grateful to eventually progress to "front door entry!"

Both Cindy and I were relieved to finally look normal again and I still remember that struggle together, and after that I don't remember ever getting any strawberries off those plants!

In summary, these are the stories of a family, bound together by experiences that have nurtured love and support for each other. We are like any other family in that we have had challenges and rewards, peace and strife, teamwork and competitiveness, joy and grief. That we can say we are a family is the blessing. That we were given the opportunity to have these experiences together is the gift for which I am most grateful. My parents provided a home where we were able to firmly plant our roots. They sustained us with faith, love, prayers, structure and discipline, providing a secure point from which to grow and venture out into the world. No matter how far away we may ramble, our roots will also remain . . . at home!

Eddie

My dad planted soybeans in some acreage on the farm, and we kids were sent out during the summer months to pull and destroy the pigweeds which were growing faster than the soybeans. Now, if you have never heard of a pigweed, I can assure you that you are forever blessed. The only thing worse than a pigweed is a yellow fly. The yellow flies somehow liked my deodorant or hair do and were very persistent. It was the only insect I ever met that would make an unprovoked aggressive attack and the more you swatted them the madder and more aggressive they got. There were only two things I found would stop a yellow fly attack: 1) kill them, and 2) a direct hit with a healthy dose of insect spray. So, I always carried around a can of Raid with me any time I was pulling pigweed.

My name is Eddie, and I am the next to oldest son. Dad had asked me several times to haul off a stray cat or dog that had wandered into the yard and wanted to stay. One day, a large stray dog appeared at the back door. My training took over, and I put the dog into the car and drove it several miles down the road. Unfortunately, this particular dog was Uncle T's new prize dog that he had apparently spent real money on (I didn't know at the time that people actually paid for dogs). We searched for Uncle T's dog for several hours to no avail. It was never seen again. To my surprise, Dad didn't ask me to go over to Uncle T's and take the blame for what I had done. He went over and told Uncle T himself.

Another time we noticed a stray dog in our yard, and, wishing to be obedient I put him in the car and carried him a safe distance from our home. When I returned home I was surprised to find the same dog sitting on the back steps! Smart dog.

I decided I wanted my freedom, so I set out with my parents' permission to graduate after my junior year of high school so I could go to college a year early. I took several classes that were populated by seniors and in my own mind (and only in my mind), I had elevated myself to senior status since that was my last year of high school. One day a senior field trip was planned and I lined up to get on the bus for the field trip with the rest of the seniors. The principal pulled me out of line as I was stepping up into the bus and asked me where I thought I was going. I explained to him that this was my final year; therefore, I should be able to go on the senior trip. He had a different opinion on the matter and told me I was not going. Fuming mad, I got in my car and drove home. Dad met me at the door and asked what I was doing home so early. I explained what had happened and my frustration with the principal. Dad calmly told me that he thought I should go back to school and attend my classes for the rest of the day, and we would discuss it further when I got home. By the time I got home, the crisis was over, and I had calmed down and moved on to other things. His calm conversation with me after the incident, and his advice about what to do was a great piece of parenting.

During college I grew accustomed to sleeping late whenever I could, so coming home for the summer was quite a shock. My sisters were always up early performing their Saturday morning chores. The first few days of my summer break, I could hear them scheming outside my closed door to determine who got the pleasure of coming in with the vacuum cleaner and waking me up.

I was quite proud of the fact that I knew more about pretty much everything than any of my sisters. On a trip in the station wagon to Clemson with Polly, we had a flat tire. I boastfully told her to stand back and observe the proper procedure for changing a flat tire. I pulled the bumper jack out (which I had never actually seen or used before) and proceeded to use it as a scissor jack on the side of the car instead of the bumper. When used in this unorthodox manner, the jack will put a nice vertical dent in your fender and will become stuck. When this happens the release mechanism that allows it to go down no longer works. We ended up having to go door to door until we found a stranger to help us get the stuck jack released. I later had to explain to Dad why we came home with a nice sized dent in the rear car fender. Although Polly never mentioned the incident to me again, I'm sure she gleefully shared the story of my gloating and subsequent humiliation with all of my other sisters.

I was working at the IGA grocery store, and for those patrons who walked to the store because they didn't have a vehicle, we were asked to use our vehicles to deliver them and their groceries to their homes. Some of these folks smoked and left cigarette butts in the ash trays in the car. I had to explain to Mom why there were cigarette butts in the ash trays of the car I had been driving. I was never completely sure she believed my explanation. If I had only been able to get her to realize how much of an influence watching my Granddaddy Carter die from smoking cigarettes had on me when I was a little boy, she would have known she never had to worry about me becoming a smoker. I had many friends in middle and high school who smoked and wanted me to join them. I never did, not even once!

My cousin, Keith Sutcliffe, and I liked driving Dad's Volkswagen bug down the dirt road and goosing it around corners so we would get a little extra slide in the loose sand. One day, I cut it a little too hard and it went into a spin. When it finally came to a stop, we were turned around 180 degrees and headed the other way. I never tried that stunt again!

One of my buddies showed me how to down shift the manual transmission to slow the Volkswagen down when taking corners. This sounded and felt really "cool", kind of like a race car driver, so I started taking turns this way. It didn't take long for Dad to notice, which led to a chat about how downshifting ruins the clutch prematurely. So, I was quickly back to slowing down using the uncool brake method.

Poor Mom and Dad had to teach eight of us to drive. One day Mom was letting me drive, and I didn't understand how to judge when it was safe to pull out across a lane of oncoming cars at an intersection and when it was not. Initially, being the daredevil that I was, I would pull out right in front of cars and see how fast I could get out of their way. This led to horn blowing, and a very unhappy driving instructor. After being chastised several times for nearly killing both of us, I got the message and started waiting until there were no cars in sight. Although this made driving a lot less nerve racking for Mom, the cars behind me didn't appreciate my newfound caution and would blow the horn for us to move. Subsequently I got chastised for waiting too long to make my turns. So, which is it Mom, do you want me to clear the intersection, or do you want me to be cautious? I didn't understand at the time that there was a happy medium to be found.

I was determined not to let Polly who was three months my senior, outdo me at anything. Being older, she was ready to take her driving road test sooner than I was. Not to be outdone, I pleaded with

Mom and Dad to allow me to take the road test as well. Although they both told me I wasn't ready to take the test, they allowed me to try anyway. I hadn't been driving for more than a minute when the officer in the seat beside me asked me how fast I was going. I looked at the speedometer and said, "47 miles per hour". He then asked me what the speed limit was, to which I shrugged my shoulders because observing speed limit signs was something I hadn't learned yet. He informed me the speed limit was 35 miles per hour. He allowed me to drive a little farther and half way into the parallel parking test, he asked me to return to the DMV. We then sat in the parking lot for a long time as he read out every infraction I had made during the test. He said I was spinning my tires before I even left the parking lot, followed by accelerating to the point where I was 12 miles per hour over the speed limit, and this was less than 60 seconds into the test. Needless to say, I failed the test. Much to my chagrin, Polly passed with flying colors.

There was a division of chores in our house, where the girls did the cooking and helped Mom with the laundry, and the guys did the trash, auto work and dog feeding. One unfortunate consequence of this division of labor was that I never learned to do laundry. I didn't know how to separate darks from lights from brights. I didn't know how long you could sleep on sheets before they needed to be washed. And I didn't know what types of clothes can go through the washer and dryer and what types can't.

Subsequently, as a freshman at Clemson, laundry day was always an adventure. I routinely pulled multicolor shirts out of the dryer that went in as a single color. One fall day, the weather turned cool, and I noticed all of my sweaters were smelling a little musty, so I decided to wash them. Imagine my surprise when I pulled each one out of the dryer at the end of the cycle to find the sleeves were now four feet long and the bodies were three feet wide and eight inches high. I managed to destroy an entire wardrobe of sweaters in a single washing.

Like any child, there were foods that I had decided I did not like.

Sometimes it wasn't that the foods actually tasted bad to me, but that I had just randomly decided that I did not like them. Cheese was one of those foods. I declared one day that I did not like cheese of any kind. Mom and I were at Tony's Pizza one day ordering pizzas to eat in the car. I told her that I didn't care what kind of pizza she ordered so long as it didn't have cheese on it. She said fine, and went in to order the pizzas. A few minutes later she came back out with two pizzas that were both delicious and were quickly devoured by the two of us. When we had finished the last slice, she asked me if I enjoyed the pizza, to which I said that they were really super great. She then replied, "I'm so glad you liked them because they were both loaded with cheese!" I was a little mad, but the lesson was made and I never turned my nose up at cheese again.

To this day, I have no idea how Mom and Dad stretched their income far enough to feed and clothe eight children plus themselves, make house payments, and keep the lights on. Finding inexpensive foods that would go a long way was likely one of their strategies. One day, they hit on a new cost saving food that I had never heard of before, creamed beef. I thought I would give it a try until I caught sight of it in the pot cooking. I won't say what it looked like to me, but the sight of it made me a little nauseous. I declared that I could not and would not eat the creamed beef. I was told that was fine so long as I was okay going hungry until the next morning. I gladly took the starvation option. To this day, I don't think I ever tried the creamed beef.

Another cost saving option was to eat foods from the garden in summer, and can/freeze garden foods for the winter. I was expected to participate in the food gathering and preparation. I begrudgingly went along until we got to the butter bean shelling. I absolutely hated shelling butter beans. I would shell for what seemed like hours only to look down at the small amount of beans this produced – barely enough for one person for one meal. I agreed that butter beans were delicious, but the quantity of beans produced per hour of shelling was just too low to make it worthwhile. Although I made sure my displeasure did not go unnoticed, I was never clever enough to finagle myself out of butter bean shelling.

When I was a teenager, I decided one day to make doughnuts. I had absolutely no idea how to make doughnuts, but found a recipe somewhere. I mixed the ingredients and cooked the doughnuts, which didn't turn out very well. When someone helped me review the ingredients, we discovered I had forgotten to add the flour.

One food that I did like was banana pudding. One day while at Clemson, I decided to make some. Following a recipe that I had found, it said I was to make a topping for the pudding out of egg whites. After separating the whites from the yokes, I was to beat the whites until they formed "peaks." I had never heard this term before, so I beat the egg whites for a while with a fork and noticed when I removed the fork, the egg whites followed the fork out for a while before letting go. I figured this was the "peaks" the recipe was referring to. I then poured the egg whites on top of the banana pudding and put it back in the oven. I was very disappointed when I removed the pudding a few minutes later to find it covered by a funny layer of uncooked egg whites.

My time at home in the Sutcliffe household was cut a little short because of my early graduation from high school. Yet, I am who I am today largely because of the values and religious training I learned while living in a family of 10. I am forever grateful to be a part of this family.

Julie

Well, I'm Julie. Somewhere along the way I graduated from being the one who got in trouble to the one who gets things done. I guess that's a good thing. Growing up in a family where we transitioned from it being just Dad and five children to having a new mom and three more siblings did present its challenges. But I cannot imagine it happening any other way now. It's made me who I am today. It's made me determined and steadfast in the face of change. And a part of a family who loves and sacrifices and holds each other in the good times and the bad. Here are a few of my childhood memories. Yeah, when I was good. AND the parts when I just couldn't help myself!

One afternoon we were sitting in the den after the lunch dishes had been all cleaned and put away. My sister, Janet, was sitting across the room. Janet was usually very quiet, but this particular evening she said something that just made me mad. And she wouldn't stop. She was getting so mad at my retorts in her direction. Suddenly, she picked up a pair of cuticle scissors and with one swift launch, the scissors whizzed through the air and stuck me right at my hairline. I wailed and my sister, Polly, came running and removed the cuticle scissors from my head and quickly soothed my cries. Janet jumped up to see if I was alright and quickly said she was sorry. Janet just knew she was going to get in trouble this time. Polly must have worked some magic that day, because neither Mom nor Dad ever found out about the incident. Later that night at the table when we all sat together for supper, I looked at Janet and rubbed my forehead, moving my bangs to the side so someone else might notice the marks left by the scissors. Janet shifted in her seat and must have begged God to keep me from spilling the beans, which would mean another spanking for her for sure. But I didn't say a word. I must have decided to give her some grace.

Christmas was an exciting time! I always loved putting up the tree and adding the decorations. But sometimes my curiosity got the best of me. Seeing all of the presents pile up under the tree peaked my interest 'til I just couldn't wait until the 25th. Late at night when everyone had gone to bed, I'd sneak in the den, look for several of my presents, and take my loot back to my bedroom. Quiet as a mouse, I'd carefully unwrap the gifts to reveal the treasures. Now, Cindy and I were close in age, and we usually got the same presents. Cindy and I shared a bedroom, so as I unstuck the tape and opened each gift, Cindy was awake during these adventures. Cindy liked surprises, and didn't want to know about our Christmas bounty. As I opened each present, I just couldn't help but tell her all about the contents, describing each in full detail. She would put her hands over her ears, trying not to hear, but it was no use. Of course, we acted surprised and delighted on Christmas morning. There were usually a few gifts that I hadn't sabotaged, so we did get some surprises!

It was no secret that I detested working in the garden. We kids all had to help with pulling weeds, picking a smorgasbord of vegetables, and then freezing or canning our harvest in the kitchen. But I hated picking butterbeans the worst of all. Cindy and I would lie in bed at night scheming how to kill the plants, and ease our toils every day during the summer. We picked a lot while Mom and Dad were at work. I really don't know how in the world we accomplished a lot, except that we better have a considerable amount picked by the time Daddy got home from work. While picking beans one day, I decided to act on my covert operation. About every fifth bush, I'd pull on it enough to dislodge the roots. Then every tenth bush, I'd pull it all of the way out the ground! I never told anyone about my strategy to lower the bean population. It made me feel like I was helping everyone else out, even if they didn't know it!

One summer afternoon, I fell asleep on a sofa in the den. "Perfect Polly" (She rarely did anything wrong!) snuck up and cut part of my bangs so short, dippity doo wouldn't even lay them down. I was so mad. I didn't raise too much of a stink, but thought to myself "I'll get you back, Sista." I told Cindy, "Let's sneak down the hall really late while everyone is asleep. I'm gonna cut Polly's hair this time." Somehow I talked Cindy into coming with me on my midnight expedition. We tip-toed through the house towards Polly's bedroom. I turned the knob to open her door and immediately heard the cow bell ringing like a clanging cymbal. I quickly closed the door, and we started running back to our bedroom. I ran into the sharp corner of our oak table, and felt my hip bone sending pain signals all through my body. I was snickering, all the while rubbing my poor pelvic bone. Through the darkness, I looked up and saw my dad standing in front of me like a giant.

"What's going on here?"

"Nothing," I said, holding the scissors behind my back. Polly appeared in her nightgown, and said, "She was gonna cut my hair!"

"Y'all go on back to bed. And stay in your beds," Dad commanded.

We all scampered back to our bedrooms. I don't know about Polly. But Cindy and I laughed and talked about our midnight adventure 'til our eyes finally gave way to slumber.

My sister Cindy and her best friend decided to cut school one day. Of course, the school administrators found out and she was called into the office. For once, it wasn't me getting into trouble! But, I hated it for her. Our friends tried to talk Cindy into intercepting the notice of detention at the post office. Which was intended for our parents. She was suspended from school for three days, and to add to the embarrassment Dad was called by the school principal to explain Cindy's suspension. In addition to having her license taken for six weeks, Mom made Cindy read a lengthy book and write a full book report. Graded by Mom. With her red, editing pen. I really did feel sorry for Cindy then.

Occasionally Mom and Dad would treat us to a trip to McDonalds. My younger sister, Janet, was a picky eater and would usually leave half of her cheeseburger uneaten. I used this to my advantage on more than one occasion, as I had a pretty good appetite. I told her as we were piling into the station wagon, "You better leave half of your burger for me." We all went into the restaurant and enjoyed our fast food meal. I watched Janet munch away, as she devoured every single morsel of her burger. I got so mad at her. She just smiled at me while rubbing her stomach! Another time, we were up at my Grandmomma Sutcliffe's house. My grandma would take bananas and put them in the freezer 'til they got nice and firm. Then, she'd put the frozen banana on a stick, roll it in peanut butter, and top it off with crunchy nuts. Janet was also up at Grandma's house looking forward to our treat. I told Janet, "You know you're not going to eat the whole thing. Leave most of it for me." Well Grandma overheard my comment to Janet. You didn't mess with Grandma, now. She told me to sit at the table while Janet got her banana dessert. "Today, Miss Julie, you're not going to get one," she said.

And I was to watch Janet eat the whole thing! I sat there fuming, but really thinking that Grandma would cave and finally give me one. She held firm, and the most enjoyment I got that day was just salivating as I watched Janet take slow bites of a sticky, delicious banana treat.

Later when Grandmomma Sutcliffe got sick, she came to stay with Mom and Dad. At that time, I was studying to be a Licensed Practical Nurse. Grandma spent most of her day resting in a hospital bed. Hospice nurses and my parents ministered to Grandma during her last days. One afternoon I decided to bring my notes and study while sitting on a stool in Grandma's room. She had been sleeping most of the day, but suddenly opened her eyes out of the clear blue and said, "If you're gonna sit there all day, you need to go put some make-up on and fix your hair." I just had to smile. She never did mince words and told it like it was.

Our bedroom was right next to Linnie and Eddie's room. Eddie had a small television and they loved to watch episodes of Mash at night. Cindy and I would lie in bed just about to fall asleep when we'd hear Eddie's laughter ringing out about something Radar or Hot Lips or some other Mash character was saying. Sometimes we'd hear Linnie and Eddie roaring with laughter especially after eating beans or some other food that caused eruptions all during the night hours!

Our large family traveled in a Ford station wagon. The older kids got to enjoy riding in the seats while us younger ones had to endure the rear and the well seats at the very end of the vehicle. We always looked forward to our older siblings going off to college so we could graduate to a seat towards the front. Then, we could see where we were going instead of where we'd been.

I visited Cindy at her home in Orangeburg before Dad married. Cindy's family had a housekeeper named Annie Mae Pair. Cindy loved Annie Mae, and told me she would feign sickness to stay home from school with her to play crazy eights or watch soap operas in the afternoons. One day while I was at Cindy's house, Annie Mae was watching "All My Children". One of the characters was letting a bad guy have it and Annie Mae jumped up and down yelling, "Get him, get him!" I thought I felt the house shake that day. Cindy came to visit me at our home in Norway shortly after my dad and her mom started dating. She got out of the car that day, looked around the property seeing nothing but fields and acres of crops and said, "Where are the stores?" I laughed at this "city girl" and wondered how in the world she would make it here in the country.

I'm sure there are many other memories of my childhood days growing up in a new family of ten. These are the ones that play over and over in my mind these days. During that time when Dad married and I got a new mom and three new siblings, there were some tough, hard days. But you know what? I felt safe. I felt loved. I still do. And I'm who I am today because of every single struggle.

Cindy

My name is Cindy. And here are a few memories about a family merger that would forever change the course of my life.

Even as a young, tender, preteen girl, I realized the enormous void felt after the sudden death of my dad, Edward Carter. I missed my daddy's laugh, his smile, and watching our housekeeper, Annie Mae, wake my dad's slumber after working the night shift as a police officer in Orangeburg, South Carolina. The word "Daddy" was abruptly removed from my lips, and I secretly wondered if I'd ever utter it again. My dad's mangled jeep was a reminder of the accident that tragically took his life as he traveled home late one night in November.

After four years, my mom began dating a man, Linnie Sutcliffe, from Norway, South Carolina. They began seeing each other more frequently, and I noticed Mom's face light up when he came into our home. I could hear laughter and muted conversations as they sat together in our den. I saw my mom transformed into a happy woman again, and it made me happy, too. Mr. Linnie had five children, and if I ever asked about them, he'd proudly pull out pictures and start naming them all, telling me their names and ages.

One daughter, Julie, was one year older than me. Mom arranged for Julie to come visit me for a weekend. Julie seemed so grown up! She knew about Donnie Osmond and other pop stars. She was tall, had dark hair, and I felt instantly hip in her presence. We talked until the wee hours of the morning, and I had a ball with my new friend! Mom took me to Norway to spend the weekend with Julie on another occasion, and I got to experience country living. We played outside in her enormous yard, and I loved being around her brother and sisters. It was like being at a youth camp!

Well, after Mom married Linnie Sutcliffe, as you can imagine, my life drastically changed. Transported to the countryside, living in a strange house with new siblings, and given chores to do every day, I fell right into line and did as I was told. But, I secretly longed for my neighborhood friends back in Orangeburg, and our afternoon escapades up and down the street.

Before our move to Norway, my friends and I formed clubs. Our club decided that all of the neighborhood dogs attached to leashes or in cages needed to be set free. We walked from yard to yard opening pet enclosures and releasing dogs from their "prisons". Some of the dogs followed us around, and we marched like soldiers setting captives free. I don't remember hearing any discussion about so many dogs roaming the neighborhood that particular summer, and we never did get caught. Our club gained new members, and our ventures took a more ominous turn. Several of my friends sneaked cigarettes and lighters from their parents, and we began smoking in the woods. We would send the oldest club member into the Seven-Eleven store to buy cigarettes. To this day, I cannot believe that a clerk would allow a child to purchase cigarettes. But it happened!

We continued to smoke in our woody hide-out, feeling liberated and free. Somehow Mom learned about my smoking and confronted me one night at supper. She cried and explained that smoking was very addictive. Her face was tired and red from heavy sobbing. I promised that day never to smoke again, mostly because I saw my mom's spirit crushed like never before.

After Mom's marriage and our move to Norway, Mom retained our home in Orangeburg for a time, and rented it to supplement income. While some renovations were being done to the rental home, it was revealed that my friends had vandalized several rooms, leaving trash, and evidence of smoking and urine on the hard wood floors. I was horrified, and it hurt.

"How could they? My friends?"

Mom eventually decided to sell our Orangeburg home, and finally close that chapter in our lives. Surprisingly, I was relieved for my mom and for me, that my so called "friends" wouldn't cause any more stress and hardship on my family. Several years later as I matured and developed a new understanding about God's mysterious workings in my life, I realized that Mom's marriage and our move to Norway was a pivotal season in my life as a budding teen. I believe if we had stayed in Orangeburg, I would have followed my rebellious friends into all sorts of trouble.

As much as I struggled at times to adjust to my new home and surroundings in the country after Mom's marriage, I learned so much about cooperation, being responsible with assigned chores, and doing hard work. And at the same time my heart grew more in tune with the Lord, seeking His blessing and will for my life. I couldn't imagine living anywhere else.

My brother, Mark, and I could be found any given day, playing outside with his vast collection of matchbox cars and trucks, and bulldozers. We'd use rakes and shovels to create hills, tunnels, and a complex network of roads in the soft, dark soil. The lush foliage of enormous pecan trees provided shade for our summertime adventures in the country. For a time during the first summer and fall as a new family, Mark and I continued to closely play together. It didn't take long though for us to blend into the fold of our newly formed family of ten. By the next summer, all four younger siblings (Janet, Julie, Mark and I) could be found down by the creek, walking the dirt road, or planning adventures right in our own back yard. I quickly learned that our entire family was faced with the task of weeding, harvesting, and preserving vegetables and fruits from my dad's garden. I mean not just any garden. I'm talking a gargantuan cornucopia of tomatoes, peas, okra, butter beans, peppers, onions, potatoes, corn, scuppernongs, and whatever seed my dad could find to feed our family. And really not just for our consumption, but also because he absolutely loved watching plants grow.

I could not in my wildest dreams understand why any human being would want to sweat bullets in a garden for ANY reason. My single job before moving to Norway was to unload the dishwasher. That's it. So, I was definitely in for a rude awakening! My new Grandma Sutcliffe also had a garden, and we kids helped harvest her veggies, too. I'd trudge up to her house with my siblings, dreading the long, hot business of digging potatoes, shucking corn, or sitting under the trees snapping beans for hours on end. She was always so happy during those times, whether bent over picking produce, raking, or shelling those pointed, "hard to shell" butter beans. I never once heard her complain or speak of an aching back, as she worked right along beside us.

"This won't take long," she'd say. We'll be done in no time."

Her spirit often lifted ours, and we'd end up laughing and talking about her days caring for patients at a nearby nursing home. She helped us on many occasions rinse vegetables, blanch, and cool our produce before bagging them for the freezer. She, along with my mom, showed us how to can beans and prepare a variety of fruit preserves. One crop of veggies rolled right into another, and my sister, Julie, and I both shared our distaste for garden work. We'd lie in bed at night scheming how to destroy all of Dad's glorious plants.

"There's a can of gasoline in the shop," Julie said.

"Yeah," I'd add. "Let's get some matches and set the whole thing on fire. I can see it now, all those beans just burnin' up! We'll slip out there during the night so no one will see," I snickered.

Julie added, "Can't you just see the look on everybody's face? Are you kidding me? You know the rest of them will be glad, too!"

We laughed and planned and imagined the outcome, until our sleepy eyes finally closed in slumber. Well, you know it! We found ourselves right back in the garden the next day. One hot, steamy July afternoon while toiling in the garden, I stood up from plucking string beans and proclaimed with exasperation, "I will NEVER marry a farmer!" Everybody stopped picking for a brief moment, surprised that their quiet, demure sister had made such a loud declaration. I saw smirks on their faces, and everybody laughed. Then we all returned to the task at hand, and kneeled down to finish as quickly as possible.

Well, years later I fell in love with a dark, handsome man from Fountain Inn, South Carolina. And do you know his occupation? You guessed it. A farmer! A man who loved to watch things grow, who dug in the soil searching for sprouted seeds, who worked from sun up to sun down.

We eventually married on a scorching, humid day in July, similar to the sizzling days I experienced in the vegetable fields as a teenager. And incidentally, the air conditioner malfunctioned that day in our country church, and we exchanged "I do's" while blowing away gnats, JUST like I did in our garden. My husband not only planted row crops, but later raised hogs, and eventually became a poultry farmer. My husband, a man steeped in a strong work ethic, who enjoyed the outdoors, watching things grow, and who deeply but quietly displayed a love for God. My husband, a man very much in every way just like my new dad, the gardener. Now, tell me God doesn't have a sense of humor?!?

Dad placed bee hives at the lower end of the front yard. When the honey was ready to be harvested, Dad would put on his "bee clothes" and rob the hives. We children would watch from a safe distance, as our dad moved in and out of the bee area, gathering sleeves from the hive like a cloaked thief. We would all be tasked with helping to squeeze honey through cheese cloth, pouring it in jars, swatting at pesky bees who slipped inside during the honey extraction process, and of course cleaning up the sticky residue left behind. Honey was used to sweeten recipes and pour over hot, homemade biscuits. My brother, Linnie, and Dad loved eating honey, but I never did develop a liking for the golden nectar.

One summer day, I was cutting grass and steered the lawn mower towards the front yard. Unknowingly, I got too close to the bee hives. Several angry bees got caught in my long, brown curly locks. I jumped off of the mower, ran towards the house with my head upside down, swinging my arms, and screaming hysterically. I could hear the bees angrily buzzing, and I imagined that thousands of bees were preparing to sting every hair follicle on my head. My brothers and sisters were bent over laughing as I turned the corner of the house screaming, "Bees are in my hair, bees are in my hair!" Julie scanned my hair for bees, as I stood there panting. I could feel my heart pounding in my chest like a drum.

"They're all gone," Julie shrugged. "Flip your hair over." Dad, who was standing nearby, said, "They would not have bothered you, Cindy, if you'd stayed out of their flight path." I thought about it for a minute, and then replied, "How in the world do I know where their flight path is?" Dad cracked a smile, shook his head, and walked towards the barn.

I never did get stung, thank goodness! And from that day on I avoided the bee hive area completely. Who's to know a bee's flight path? My siblings love to tell that story to this day.

For a while Dad planted soybeans, and after working all day, he'd lead the way to show us how to pull pigweeds. It was hot, tiring work, and I detested working in the fields. "Turn the roots upside down so they won't keep growing," Dad reminded. We'd pull and flip. Pull and flip. Every now and then Julie and I paired up to pull some pigweeds that at the time loomed as tall as trees. "Somebody missed those last time. Pull them when they're little, and you won't have that trouble," Dad would say.

Many times we'd end up laughing as we fell to the ground attempting to uproot the enormous weeds. We laughed so hard one day, I wet my pants. Chores that I despised really weren't that bad with brothers and sisters around to talk to and find something to laugh about.

Dad also planted hay, and we all chipped in to help with harvesting and storing yet another crop. Dad drove the hay harvester and we helped load bales of hay into the barn. I remember dodging wasp nests while hoisting heavy bales from the truck onto the barn shelves. We'd ride on the back of the truck, singing songs and shooing flies and gnats away with our gloves. Until Dad would say, "Alright now, let's get to work." Then, we'd get down to business. I also remember picking cantaloupe on a nearby farm with my sister, Julie. We earned extra money that summer, working in the afternoons for a local farmer. I learned to distinguish ripe cantaloupe, to load them in sacks, throw the cumbersome pack over my shoulders, and deposit them in a truck bound for the market. I never did love working on that farm, either, but I sure did like having extra money in my pocket.

One day, I opened the closet and found my guitar, still in a soft, black case, pushed behind my ever expanding wardrobe. Before Mom remarried, she had presented me with a guitar, and at that time, I rode my bicycle several blocks to take lessons from a retired band teacher, Mr. Pop Gentry. I learned several major chords, to strum, and memorized how to play several folk songs. Mr. Pop encouraged me to play between lessons, but I rarely did. I was too busy playing with Barbies, brushing my hair, or roaming the neighborhood with my close group of friends. So, after discovering my guitar tucked away in my closet, I removed it from the case, gingerly strummed and twisted my fingers over the frets and strings to play songs etched in my memory.

Mr. uncle, Burdell Sutcliffe, taught me how to tune the strings and I soon practiced and practiced for hours after my chores were completed. My sister, Polly, also developed an interest in playing the guitar, and we'd play some together. While gathered around the sink washing mountains of dirty dishes, we sisters would sing and break off into parts of tenor, alto, and mixed harmonies. It absolutely made the dish washing chore enjoyable, and we bonded as sisters standing around the sink, passing pots, pans, cups, and plates to cupboards and kitchen shelves. We melded our voices together and had the best time coming up with moving parts to many, many songs. Around that time, I started writing poems and composed simple songs. I dreamed of singing solos just like I'd seen my mom do numerous times in church. But my shyness prevented me from acting on my secret, inner longings.

I saved my allowance money for months and purchased song books and an electric guitar and an amp from the Sears and Roebuck catalog. I continued to hone my guitar playing skills and filled my notebook with newly penned songs. I found my creative outlet, my natural bend, and music became a fresh source of joy during my life as a teenager in Norway. Listening to Karen Carpenter on the radio, I longed to one day record songs, and be an entertainer. I wanted to inspire people with my songs. I sang in my bedroom though, and refused to sing in public. Over a long period of time, I reluctantly accepted invitations to sing and play for a few church sponsored events. Polly and I sang for our sister, Julie's wedding, and even though I had extreme stage fright, I loved the experience and wanted to sing and perform again.

At the end of my freshman year in college, I met Chuck McKeowen. We dated a few times during the summer, and when I returned to Winthrop in the fall, Chuck drove up for a Saturday visit. He saw my guitar propped in the corner and asked if I'd play and sing him a song. Spreading my song book out to follow the chords and words, I quietly sang him a song that I'd been practicing for weeks. I looked up and saw him smiling. I couldn't believe it. He liked it! Well, Chuck asked me to sing on many other occasions, too.

And gradually, I was relaxed and looked forward to his requests to play and sing. Chuck and I got married at the end of my junior year in college. He encouraged me to not only sing for him, but to sing in church. I wrote love songs to him, and I also wrote about my love for my Lord and Savior. After I denied many requests to sing from leaders in our church, Chuck spoke up. "Cindy, if you don't use the music God has given you, He may take it away. He's given you this gift. You need to sing." His words came down like daggers, and they had a life altering impact. From that point on, I swallowed my fear and started on a journey of trusting God to use my music and voice. Encouraged daily by Chuck and bolstered by the strength of the Holy Spirit, I accepted the call to sing.

Slowly I emerged as a more confident instrument of God to minister with creativity, passion and power. As a Christmas gift, shortly into our marriage, Chuck presented me with a gift certificate to record songs at a nearby studio. We went together, and I recorded several praise songs that year. David Durr, the studio owner, encouraged me to spend more time writing and composing songs. After our children were born, Chuck would take all three of our youngsters on many Sunday afternoons so that I could devote time to brainstorming, practicing, and perfecting songs I'd written. Well, I went on to record THREE projects, two recordings of original works and one of Christmas songs for the holidays. The Lord has opened doors for me to share the gift of music and also share my testimony to countless churches and groups of men, women and children. Talk about a dream coming true! All because my mom presented me with a guitar. All because I witnessed her singing and wanted to be just like her!

Music discovered in an instrument found deeply buried in a closet after a life altering move to Norway. Music born out of a difficult transition in a new, blended family. Music sung while washing and drying dishes around a deep, farm sink. Music penned while deeply in love. Music composed with the enduring encouragement from my beloved husband, Chuck. Music written in my head while riding in a boat, cutting the grass, or bathing children. And music gifted by a Lord, who empowers me to this day, to sing for His glory.

Mom led a Training Union class for the youth at our church. I secretly loathed having my mom as a teacher at church. A budding adolescent, I wanted to stretch my wings and be released from the endless rules and procedures that were a hard but necessary component of living in a large, blended family. And I really didn't want for my mom to be our youth leader, imposing MORE direction in my life! As much as I dreaded those Sunday night Training Union sessions, I learned so much about the Bible under my mom's direction. I memorized scripture, heard biblical principles explained, and somewhere along the way formed a sweet relationship with Christ, my Savior and Lord. I believe my mom was a powerful instrumental force in leading me right into the arms of Jesus and cultivating a heart for wanting to know Him more and more.

Mom taught me how to sew many of my clothes. I remember going to the fabric store with several sisters and picking out our solids, florals and prints for Easter outfits. Mom would painstakingly sew and create dresses, skirts, blouses and jackets from patterns we selected. She took the time to show Julie and me how to stitch straight seams, clip corners, hem pants, use a tape measure, and iron on interfacing. Julie and I also practiced sewing in a home economics course at school, but our mom was the one who really showed us the ins and outs of sewing a variety of clothes. One of the sewing instruments I utilized a lot was the ripper. As carefully as I'd follow the instructions and sew the pieces of fabric together, there would be a mistake, and I'd reach for the ripper again and again. Over time, I made huge improvements. I eventually sewed skirts, shorts and jackets with shoulder pads and lining.

"Follow the instructions, Cindy," Mom would say. "Don't be in such a hurry."

That particular summer, Julie's boyfriend was having a pool party at his home, and invited our entire youth group. I was excited and really wanted to wear a new, two piece suit. We had some stretchy, white fabric that I thought would be perfect for a bathing suit. I cut out the pieces, and carefully read each step to assemble my tailor made bikini. Nonetheless, I skipped the important step to include interfacing.

"I don't want it to feel bulky," I reasoned.

Later at the pool gathering, I dropped my towel and joined everybody in the pool having a glorious time. After splashing and laughing with my friends, our leader said, "Y'all come on. The burgers are ready!"

One by one my friends exited to eat burgers and chips. I glanced down to check my suit before climbing the pool steps. Horrified, I saw a dark, shadowy area exactly where I should have placed INTERFACING! "What am I going to do?" I thought. "Please, Lord, just let me die right now!" My face flushed to crimson red, my heart pulsing wildly in my chest. "Everyone will see, and I'll be the laughing stock of the party." Frozen, I refused to leave the pool. "Why didn't I sew interfacing in this stupid suit?"

"Yeah, Cindy, you just HAD to wear this homemade two piece," I punished myself inwardly. A friend called out, "Cindy, aren't you going to get something to eat?" I trudged to the deep end of the pool, and camped out there for a long time, trying to discern how not to call attention to myself. I evaded all attempts to get me out of the pool to come and eat with my friends. Julie walked towards me and asked, "What's the matter, Cindy?" I turned to face my sister, and she looked down at my white swim suit and immediately realized my dilemma.

"Oh my gosh," Julie said, putting her hand to her mouth.

"Don't say anything, please," I responded. She ran towards a chair and retrieved a towel. "Here, take this and just wrap it around you, while you're coming up the steps," Julie added. "Just act like nothing is wrong."

I exited the pool with minimal embarrassment and kept the towel to cover the bottom portion of my suit for the rest of the party.

That evening as we drove home, my siblings burst out laughing at the predicament I'd faced in the pool. I laughed, too, but couldn't wait to get out of that wet, disgraceful suit. We walked in the house, still laughing, and I told Mom what had happened.

"Mom, I have NEVER been so embarrassed," I said. "I was so glad Julie walked over and saved my neck. "Or saved your bottom," Mom said with a grin. I continued to sew but learned to follow the directions to the letter after that fiasco.

After Thea and Polly left for college, in addition to washing, folding and sorting laundry, I helped prepare meals for our large family. Mom taught me how to cook all kinds of country fixins including gravy, ham purlieu, homemade biscuits, how to season beans with pork, and make a delectable macaroni pie.

One evening I was put in charge of cutting up and frying two chickens for supper. "Coat the pieces thoroughly with flour and put them in melted, hot Crisco," Mom said before heading off to work. "Cook the first side about 7-8 minutes and then turn to fry the other side," she instructed. "I'll be home around 5:30 p.m."

I carefully cut up the chickens, seasoned each piece and dredged them in flour. Heaving a large, black skillet from the cabinet, I placed it on the stove and scooped out an abundance of Crisco to fry up the chicken crispy and browned. When the Crisco had melted and reached a high temperature, I carefully dropped each piece in the sizzling oil. After a couple of minutes, I used a pronged fork to peek at the underside.

"Looks nice and brown to me," I said. I turned the pieces and allowed them to cook until the other side was brown and toasty. Each fried piece of chicken was placed on a paper towel lined platter. I continued until every piece was fried, and then I carefully set the chicken platter on our table.

"Hey, Dad," I said as he walked in the back door after working all day.

As was his routine, he'd go straight into his room, wash his hands and change clothes. Mom came in a little late that day, and she also breezed past to go change into comfortable clothes. Julie and Janet arranged the plates, forks, napkins and other side items for supper.

Dad liked to eat promptly after getting home, because he usually had other jobs to do around the house and farm. We finally all sat around the table, and Dad said the blessing. We started passing chicken, mashed potatoes and beans around to fix our plates and enjoy the meal. After a few short minutes, Dad took a thigh, and I heard him crunch down on my fried masterpiece. He chewed a few times, shook his head, and peered down at the cooked bird. When he laid the thigh on his plate, I saw meat, juicy and pink. I gulped and bit into my piece. In the center of my piece, there was also undercooked meat with red juices running out onto the plate. I immediately felt a huge lump form in my throat.

Everybody else at the table faced the same problem, even though my siblings ate the outer portion of crispy skin on their chicken pieces. My dad pushed his chicken to the side and ate the other sides without saying a word. I was completely devastated. Crying uncontrollably afterwards and believing I had fully disappointed my dad, I declared, "I'll never cook in that kitchen again!" Mom walked to my room and said, "Cindy, it's really okay. Next time, just make sure to fry it longer on both sides. And maybe turn the temp down so the grease won't be so hot. Daddy hasn't complained one bit," Mom reasoned. "You learn by making some mistakes." I pulled myself together and sauntered back into the kitchen to help clean up the dishes. Of course, I did cook again in our kitchen many times. Well, I had to. And I learned to become a good cook, too. I really did come to love cooking, especially when my brother, Lin, bragged about my homemade, sky high biscuits. But my sister, Julie, was the baker. She always made a cake when birthdays were celebrated. In our newly formed family, birthdays occurred every single month! Gifts were slim, but everyone always had a birthday cake with candles, thanks to Julie.

I was a quiet, introverted and submissive child for the most part.

But when confronted by my siblings or chastised by our parents I would "clam up" and give them the silent treatment. I would avoid conversational exchanges for days on end and relished the thought of punishing whoever had offended me. And for days, I wouldn't talk and resisted any attempts by others to engage me in conversations. I would shrug my shoulders and quietly walk away. "The silent treatment is on," I would muse, and I meant for the silence to sting worse each time.

One day Mom questioned me about a school matter and I bluntly answered with sarcasm. Mom yelled with exasperation and fury, "I am SO tired of tip-toeing around you, Cindy! It's like walking on glass!"

I could feel her annoyance and utter frustration. I would retreat to my room and quietly cry into my feather pillow. I can only imagine that my mom cried, too, on many occasions. I learned to "lighten up" on the silent treatment to avoid Mom's startling reply and to keep peace in the family. As an honest admission, I continued to use the silent treatment on my husband after our marriage. Many years passed before I totally learned to handle conflict and disappointment with a spirit of understanding and Christ-led responses rather than doling out the "Cindy cold shoulder treatment."

After getting my driving permit, Mom took me out one day for a driving lesson. I slipped behind the wheel, excited to drive and have more independence. It had been raining a lot, and the dirt road which I turned on was wet, puddled with water and extremely slick. I quickly bogged down in deep red mud, and after numerous tries with Mom's coaching, couldn't maneuver the car out of the mire. She told me to get out and that she'd try to get the car unstuck. Mom took the driver's seat and instructed me to get behind the car and push when she gave me the word. Mom moved the car in drive and then in reverse again. Nothing. It continued to drop, and I saw mud ease around the tire treads.

She said loudly, "Push!"

I pushed and felt the car inch up a little. She hit the gas, and mud started slinging like a torpedo, covering my hair, face, white t-shirt, legs and sandals.

I stood there frozen for a moment and saw Mom look back with amusement on her face. She began laughing, pointing to my mud covered body. I laughed so hard, my stomach started hurting. We called it quits, and I sloshed back to the house while Mom drove the car back home. I had to strip right at the back door before getting in the shower. My brothers and sisters thought it was VERY funny that Cindy, who never wanted to sweat or get dirty, was covered from head to toe in mud!

One of the cane chairs surrounding our table needed to be repaired as the strips of cane became worn and a hole widened. For several days, Dad worked in his shop to restore the chair, lacing strips of cane on the seat, sanding and carefully refinishing the oak wood to its luster. While Dad was at work one day, I wandered into his shop looking for a spade to use down by the creek. Julie waited at the door for me to retrieve the digger so we could get to the creek, create furrows, waterfalls and spend the entire afternoon playing on end. The spade was just out of my reach. My fingers stretched to grab it, and I stood on my tip toes, but I could not pull the spade from the shelf. Nearby was the chair, freshly painted with polyurethane. A perfect stool.

"Surely the finish must be dry," I reasoned. I stepped up on the chair with my flip flops and finally reached the spade. "Yes!"

Julie and I shut the barn door and walked towards the creek with plans to play all day.

Later that evening, while we ate supper, Dad said, "Who was in the shop today?" No one answered. I kept chewing, trying not to blink. Dad continued, "Somebody was in the shop today. There's a footprint on the chair I've been working on. Who was it?"

Someone said, "It wasn't me." Polly said, "I don't know Daddy." My face flushed, and I was sure everyone at the table could see the guilt on my face. I looked up, and Julie didn't flinch.

"I'll get to the bottom of this later," Dad retorted.

Mom got up from the table, and we started gathering dirty plates and cups to be cleaned. "Maybe it'll blow over," I thought. "Maybe he'll let it go. I'm safe."

My breathing returned to normal, and I even laughed with my sisters as we wiped the last forks and bowls. Nothing else was mentioned that night about the chair. I took my bath, changed into pajamas, and watched some television.

Later that evening after our family devotion, I went to my room and sat on the bed. I felt awful and was heavily convicted about lying to my dad, my mom and my family. The longer I reflected on the day's events, my dad's question about the chair and my lack of admission to the "crime", I felt sick to my stomach. My spirit was broken, and I cried into my pillow. The longer I lay there, I knew what I had to do. I had to tell the truth.

Putting on my robe, I walked towards my mom's room. "Can I talk to you, Mom?" I asked in a low voice. She walked into the kitchen and immediately saw my tear stained cheeks. "What in the world is the matter, Cindy?" she asked.

"Mom, it was me, I said. "I was the one who stepped on the chair. I didn't know it was wet. I'm so sorry! Please don't tell Dad. I'm scared!"

"Cindy, I'm glad you're telling me, but you have to tell Dad," Mom answered. I'm proud of you coming to me, and I know this is hard. But you've got to tell him and apologize."

I cried harder and felt like weights were hanging on my shoulders. Finally I said, "Alright. Is he out of the shower?"

"Yes," Mom said. I'll go tell him you want to talk to him." I walked into their room and saw my new dad seated on the edge of the bed. He was a great big man, with wide shoulders and strong, freckled hands. Mom stayed at the doorway in the shadows.

"Dad," I quietly said. "Can I talk to you?"

"Sure," he answered.

"I was the one who stepped on the chair. I'm sorry. I'm sorry I didn't tell you at the supper table tonight. I'm sorry I messed up the chair!" I was shaking and crying uncontrollably.

He looked up and said, "Well, I appreciate you telling me, Cindy. I could tell it was you by the size of the footprint. But I was waiting on you to figure out what to do. I just wanted you to tell the truth, that's all."

I hugged Dad and then hugged Mom, who was smiling with tears streaming down her face. I walked to my bedroom still crying and broken. But refreshed and relieved.

And free. My new dad, who was "tough as nails", whose discipline was stern, harsh and without fail, simply looked at me and offered just what my Lord and Savior would have done.

He offered me grace. And forgiveness when I really didn't deserve it. What a lesson I learned that night. That failure to admit is still a lie. To tell the truth. That my mom was a beautiful confidant. That my dad who loved me had responded with tenderness when all I could see in him was order and control. My heart started accepting my dad as "Daddy" that night. He became my hero as I continued to grow and truly understand the formidable task he undertook in shepherding two families into one. My daddy. He is truly a giant of a man.

Janet

Hi, my name is Janet and I'm the baby of the family, although I don't like to be called "the baby", so I'll say I'm the youngest. I've kept a diary since I was a child, and I'd like to share some of my musings with you, now that I'm an adult.

During the two years that I was without a mom, I felt lonely and confused many times. My sister, Polly, became my surrogate mom because it was she to whom I went for comfort and answers to my questions.

My mom and dad got married when I was nine years old, putting two families of ten people together. Being so small, I didn't voice any objections to their "plan", although I felt both unease and a little anxiousness. I was elated to gain two brothers and a sister but didn't really know how all of this would affect my life.

After their wedding, we all settled down to what I thought would be a continuation of how our household functioned. Boy, was I wrong! Almost immediately they placed on me a set of rules that everyone had to obey – who would feed the dogs, who would cook our meals, who would empty the trash, etc. Also, there was a special time we had to take our baths at night! We couldn't leave our rooms in the morning unless they were cleaned and the beds made. I always wondered why this rule didn't seem to apply to the older guys, but I was too little to question Daddy on this. However, as we settled into a daily routine, with everyone doing his or her share, things began to run smoothly in our home.

Before Mom and Dad married, my diet consisted of peanut butter and jelly sandwiches, macaroni pie, and cereal. Wow, was I in for a surprise! With ten people to feed, every one of us had to eat the same thing, and Mom embarked on the mission to introduce new foods to my diet. We had vegetable soup for supper one night, and I gagged. I was usually the last one to leave the table because I wasn't allowed to leave until 80% of my meal was eaten. The same thing happened with mashed potatoes and gravy on my initial exposure to them. I sat by Dad during meals and had the unfortunate accident of always spilling my glass filled with iced tea, covering the table cloth and several laps. As a child, I never said "I'm sorry" when I messed up, but through love, patience and example Mom taught me how to say it.

During my meal, I had several odd habits which bugged Mom. I cut the edges off of my pancakes and ate the center pieces. (I did not like pancakes!) When eating, I didn't like my food to touch each other, and I would eat one thing at a time. I still do that sometimes. Eddie had a harder time than anyone with new foods. When we had turnips one night, he said "Mom, I just can't eat those." Mom replied, "Just put some sugar on them and eat. That's all we are having tonight. No more food until tomorrow morning." Wow! I felt like I'd been vindicated, since it seemed like I was the only one who had trouble with this subject. So, I began to cover my turnips with sugar. It was pretty good.

Daddy had several fields of hay and my job during hay season was to walk the field and put the broken hay bales back on the next row of hay to be bailed. As I got older I would help stack the bales in the back of the truck. When all the other siblings had moved out, and it was Mark and I, Daddy would hire a couple of boys in the neighborhood. I drove the truck while the boys stacked the hay.

I began writing in my diary when I was thirteen. Mostly what I wrote about was what I saw outside of my window in the afternoons during study time, what the clouds and sky looked like whether it was raining or not. This tells you I didn't think much of study time because I hated trying to learn how to spell or do math.

When I was fourteen years old, we had two foster children, Winslow and Brenda, who came to stay with us for nine months. They were sister and brother and added two children to the four kids still at home. We started calling Winslow, "Win". Every Sunday morning when we all got ready to leave for church, Win would hide behind the sofa in the den. Daddy had to retrieve Win and carry him in the car. This went on for about three to four weeks until Daddy threatened him with very strong words. He never did it again. Mom made a precious, dotted dress with a big yellow bow in back for Brenda at Easter that year, and Brenda walked proudly into the church.

The older four kids came home from school in October to attend Thea's wedding to Bradley Mason whom she had dated for some time. With all of the kids together again, it felt almost "normal" to eat together and enjoy fellowship for a whole weekend. When the older four were at home for Thanksgiving, on Sunday afternoon, Lin, Eddie, Julie, Cindy, Mark, and the two foster kids stopped their playing and built a human pyramid. Someone snapped a picture for us and Mom still has that picture.

In June of the next year, my mom got very sick. She broke the news to us one night that she had cancer, and that her left kidney would have to be removed. We kids had many questions and fears about the unknowns following Mom's announcement. She enlisted us to all start praying for her healing. She postponed her surgery until after my sister Polly graduated from nursing school. Polly graduated on Friday night and Mom went into the hospital for surgery the next Monday. Everyone in all the churches in the area were in prayer for her. Even a friend who was in the Navy and on a submarine had his prayer group on the ship praying for her. They were all praying for a miracle.

Granddaddy Brunson, Mom's dad, passed away while she was in the hospital. I couldn't imagine how she was dealing with all that. Mom's kidney was removed, and when she came home, she couldn't do any chores around the house for four or five weeks. God healed my mom of cancer! I knew then that prayer really works!

A month after Mom's surgery, Julie got married to her school sweetheart. Mom made all of the dresses and they had a small, formal church wedding. She was gone! I was happy but sad because our home group was dwindling. No one was at home now except Mom, Dad, Cindy, Mark and me. Lin was in the Army making a living, Thea was married, Polly was a nurse making a living, Eddie was going to Italy in January to get his master's degree in architecture, and Julie was married. I was very sad because of all of the memories we had. I wanted my brothers and sisters back, but they were gone! I wondered if they ever thought about me. I wanted things to go back to how they used to be. I loved them. I wanted them back. "May God bless them," I thought. Soon I would be gone too. How would Mom and Dad feel then?

When I was fifteen and had a driver's license, I approached Mom and Dad about driving a bus to and from school. Mark had been driving a school bus for some time, and I thought it only fair to give me permission to drive, too. They talked it over and decided that I had not had enough experience driving to tackle driving a large bus full of children. I thought the decision was grossly unfair and I was angry. Looking back now, I understand their reluctance in giving me permission.

Dealing with Mark's hyperactivity was hard for me at first when the families were brought together. He could not be still and would be up and down during the night. My bedroom was near his bedroom, and he would keep me awake some nights banging his feet on the wall of his room. He got much better after he began taking medication, and Polly told me to ignore him. Mom always kept sugar away from Mark, but if he ever got a taste of powdered donuts behind her back, the problem would be tripled.

When Eddie began to drive us to school, I had a really hard time dealing with his wild driving habits. He would drive really fast around curves. One day I remember I began to cry and he pulled over, got out, and told Polly to get under the wheel so I would stop crying. No one ever told Mom! Eddie's wild driving caught up with him one day when Daddy took both him and Polly to try for their driving licenses. Polly passed the test with flying colors. Eddie? He failed before he even got out of the parking space at the highway department. The officer told Daddy when Eddie backed out, he had one hand on the wheel and the other one out the window and didn't bother to look behind him.

Dad suffered a ruptured disc and had to have back surgery. He missed about four weeks from work and had to be in his chair much of the time. We were really "on our toes" with our chores while he was recuperating!

I loved it when Linnie Jr. would come home from college to visit. He would take up many hours with me playing games such as Monopoly, Checkers, or card games. I remember many hours spent on the floor of the den building Lincoln Log homes and cities. There was nine years difference in our ages, but it never seemed to matter to Linnie Jr. and I loved him for it.

I was never a good student in school. During our study time every afternoon when we were in our rooms doing our homework,

I spent my study time dreaming and looking out my bedroom window at the dogs playing in our yard. This behavior showed up in my report cards. My mom helped me learn to spell my words every night but it didn't seem to help much. Here is my interim report in Chemistry:

> *Recent progress: poor*
> *Present status: not passing*
> *Attendance: irregular, bus driver*
> *General attitude towards work: appears to try*
> *Recommendations: increased preparation for class*

This is the note that I wrote on it - "Never showed this to Mom & Dad and more than likely, never will. Got into too much trouble last time."

(I guess since many years have passed, Mom, it's okay now for you to see this!)

After many months absence of everyone being together, we had a big dinner. All of the kids were here and I was so happy to have them all together. With only the four younger ones at home all the time, it was wonderful to have a big dinner. Everyone was here except Eddie. He was at Clemson College studying. Lin left after lunch to go back to Ft. Benning, and Cindy and Susan (her cousin) went back to Winthrop.

I finally got my driving license and Mom and Dad gave their permission for me to drive a school bus the following year, which would be my senior year. At the end of the year, I was chosen to have the honor of being the best bus driver of the year. Mom and Dad were very proud of me.

Lin left for Korea to serve for two years. I was very afraid for him after he told me of the conditions over there. He was my big brother and my checkers partner. I knew Korea was halfway around the world and I prayed for him every day.

In August, Grandma Sutcliffe and I went to Wichita, Kansas to visit my Uncle Bobby. It was the first time either of us had flown.

We had to change planes at O'Hare Airport, Chicago. Once inside the airport at O'Hare and heading to our connecting gate, Grandma would stop every person she saw in a flight uniform and ask them if we were going in the right direction. That happened about every five minutes. We got to our gate and checked in and had to wait. I asked Grandma if I could go to the bathroom. She said, "No, you can go on the plane." I was looking at the bathroom sign no more than five yards away. I pointed it out to her and she still said no and that was the end of that. No arguing with Grandma!

"The Day I Walked on Water" - One Father's Day Daddy, Mom, Polly Mark and I went to Grandma Brunson's lake house. Julie and Terry came with their ski boat. Mark did very well that day. I was finally able to stay up after my fourth try. My legs were really tired by that time. When the boat turned toward the left, my left leg gave way and that ski came off. Without thinking, I stepped forward. At that moment, my right ski came off and I stepped forward with my right foot. Again quickly I stepped forward with my left and right foot and then realized I'd better let go of the rope. Hence, "the day I walked on water." Everyone had a good laugh including me!

Lin came home from Korea in March for nineteen days and boy, was I ecstatic! We had such fun playing games and riding in his new car. I was sad again when he had to report to Ft. Benning to serve, but was excited again to see him in his Air Force uniform.

Daddy got really upset because I only made $10.22 for driving a bus of kids to camp. Daddy told Mom to tell me that I would never again drive that bus as long as I was living under his roof. He felt like I should have gotten at least $20-25 because I had all those kids' lives in my hands. I really loved driving a bus, and there would be other times that I could drive.

Mark graduated in June and left in October for basic training at Lackland Air Force Base in Texas. I was thinking of joining the Air Force after graduation. That is, if I was accepted. I was not making good grades in high school so I had my doubts. I wanted to join the Army to be like my other brother, Lin, but he told me that if I joined the Army he would break both my legs. He advised me to join the Air Force but if I wanted to go into the Army to go to college and become an officer. That wasn't going to happen, so the Air Force it was!

I think it was sometime in 1983, when Mark, my brother, was stationed in North Dakota. Mark had a truck that he wanted Daddy to sell. Daddy was outside showing the truck to a prospective buyer. The phone rang. I answered and spoke with a gentleman inquiring about Mark's truck. Leaning out of the back door, I said, "Daddy, there's a man on the phone asking about Mark's truck." Daddy told me to tell the man to hold on just a minute. When Daddy came in, he picked up the phone, and related to the gentleman that the truck had just been sold. After hanging up, Daddy said, "That was good timing, Janet. When the man outside heard that someone else was interested in the truck, he bought it right then and there." God is good, isn't He?

I must have been about 10 years old at this time. Julie was sitting in Mom's chair in front of the den window. Julie made me really mad about something and somehow I got hold of a pair of cuticle clippers, and I threw them at Julie with all the strength I could muster. The clipper stuck in Julie's forehead on her hair line. Julie started to wail, and Polly went to care for her. Mom and Dad weren't at home at the time, and I don't ever remember getting in trouble for it.

The first few years Mom and Dad were married, Mark and I would get into trouble. We played together okay but we did argue a lot. Mark was hyperactive and I didn't know how to handle him. Through love and patience Mom taught me how to ignore Mark. Once I started to learn how to ignore him, we argued less. This lesson on how to ignore someone helped me later on down the road when I went into basic training for the Air Force. The training instructors seemed to always be yelling at us airmen. I was able to ignore most of the yelling and get through basic training. To this day, if I so choose, I can ignore someone or something pretty good.

One weekend Cindy's roommate and cousin, Susan, came home with Cindy for a weekend. We were coming home from church and passed a soybean field. The leaves were just beginning to turn and Daddy made a remark that before long they would be ready to be picked. No one said anything for a minute and then Susan piped up, "Who's gonna pick all those beans?" (Susan was from Delaware and had never seen a soybean field.) Everyone in the car had a big laugh about the yankee and the soybeans!

My Last Diary Entry At Home

"The Day Your Last Child Left Home" - Off I go to basic training at Lackland Air Force Base just like Mark. The youngest, yes, the baby of the family, the spoiled one some may say. As I watched the others leave, watching their cars go down the road for as long as I could; a house of ten became quieter with the leaving of each one. But it was a Christian home I grew up in. A home where the family altar was held and the family prayed together. Some tears, many laughs, and always the unconditional love of two parents that I'm so blessed to have.

PART 3

Chapter 20

HELP!

One of the basic desires of every human being is the desire to be needed. This yearning is especially true for a woman whose nature is to be needed by those she loves and serves. I have seen many women who hold up under tremendous emotional pressure during the child-rearing years when they are serving as housewife, nurse, disciplinarian, counselor, cook, and chauffeur. This basic need is being met as a mother provides constant supervision, love, and direction for her children. Then after the children marry and establish homes of their own, these women are suddenly faced with a feeling of uselessness, and many can't cope with it. We wonder how mothers hold up all through years of juggling child rearing, keeping up with a home, meeting the needs of jobs, and financial troubles, etc. But it's during those hectic, exhausting years that women feel most fulfilled and satisfied. And sadly later, they become discouraged, unhappy and often turn to alcohol or drugs to escape their inability to handle the change.

It is a wise woman who seeks other avenues of interest when her children near maturity, such as volunteer work at a hospital, extra church activities, or organizations that can fulfill this need. After Janet, our last child, left for the Air Force, I felt "lost" for several months. It was then that I began to seek other places that I could be used to help someone else. Being a breast cancer survivor, I decided to be a volunteer in Reach to Recovery, a group of women who gave of their time to reach out to other survivors of breast cancer. I worked with this organization for about ten years until the program was canceled. Because of the wonderful care that Hospice gave to my mother-in-law when she was in our home, I then decided to work with Hospice as a volunteer, where I worked for about eight years until health issues forced me to give it up.

My only known spiritual gift given to me by the Holy Spirit is the gift of encouragement, which I began to utilize when I left Hospice and which I continue today. I mail cards and notes to shut-ins, those who are sick, hospitalized, or to friends who might need spiritual support. I also prepare meals on occasion for those who are not able to cook, and those suffering from cancer who need comfort and support. It is because of my dedication in these endeavors that I have continued to feel completely fulfilled.

Every couple experiences a period of adjustment during the first year of marriage. Linnie and I weren't immune to the problems that accompany marriage. In fact, our adjustments were more complex because of our previous marriages and the fact that there were two families involved, and ten people to be considered. We did have a traumatic first year as a couple, many times of sadness, loneliness, and soul-searching. Without God as our constant referee and counselor, we wouldn't have made it; and with Him beside us when the storms came, we emerged in a closer relationship to each other and to Him. He showed each of us our faults and shortcomings and enabled us to begin to talk openly with each other about our "hang-ups" and gripes. We needed God's hand in every part of our family, and our marriage. Every day.

Surprisingly, one of the most traumatic problems I faced as I entered into this new marriage was the lack of feeling needed. As the weeks passed and we settled into our new relationship, I began to notice that nothing ever seemed to be a problem to Linnie. Here was a totally confident individual, always having an answer to every situation. He never seemed to need my opinion, voice of experience or "shoulder to cry on." He was always on top of every situation with an answer to every problem. Whenever I would approach him in our bedroom about a problem with one of the children, he would reply, "Well, that's no problem" and proceed with his own solution, thereby minimizing the concerns I had. Without meaning to, he was eliminating my need to be a vital part of parenting and leading the family.

As the weeks and months passed, the matter worsened as I felt more and more useless in our partnership. To make matters worse, instead of telling Linnie how I felt, I kept the feeling inside, harbored it, and it began to grow into resentment.

About four months after we were married, Linnie was taking the kids to the dentist. He asked me to get off work to go with them. Julie was about due for braces and he wanted me to talk with the dentist about when we should proceed with the braces and what needed to be done. I was elated at his obvious need for me and promptly asked for time off. We arrived at the dental office, they all went in, and the dentist called Linnie back for a consultation about Julie's braces! I sat, silently fuming, for the remainder of the visit and sulked all the way home! Linnie could tell something was wrong, but he was oblivious to the reason for my attitude. "What's wrong, sweetheart?" he asked when we were in the car heading home. "Nothing", I replied curtly. I was not honest with him, which was very wrong.

I was seeking God's help in my dilemma but couldn't see the answer yet. I cried out to Him even more earnestly after that day at the dentist, knowing that the future happiness of my marriage was at stake. I couldn't let the seeds of resentment take root in my heart and grow until they choked my marriage. God was beginning to move in my life and personality in a mighty way, and slowly I began to see the answer to my cries for help in strange ways. Little did I know that God was working in Linnie's life and heart too. I began to feel that God was telling me "Be honest – don't hold feelings in where they can breed. Tell Linnie how you feel."

I argued with God for a while, saying I couldn't complain to

Linnie. He was a wonderful and devoted husband and father in every other way, I just couldn't tell him of my feelings. But the message was clear and kept returning – "Be honest, tell him." So one night I decided it was time for a "moment of truth", and I poured out my heart to my husband, unfolding all the resentment, the feelings of uselessness, not knowing if he would have a remote understanding of my problem. There were tears shed as I laid my burden in the open, praying all the while that God would help him to understand. He put his arms around me, comforting and reassuring me that he did need me very much and apologized for hurting me. God is truly in the miracle business because a miracle was performed in our marriage that night.

I began to notice that Linnie would ask my opinion about a matter of finances or a decision concerning the children. His well-known "no problem" which had become a source of irritation to me began to slip from his vocabulary. He asked me the next month to help him settle the monthly bills and to keep the checkbook up to date for him. During the farming time, he asked me to be the bookkeeper for the farm books. As time passed the wounds of resentment faded along with the problem that had caused them. Through Linnie, God healed a part of a marriage that could easily have become very "sick", had I not depended on "The Great Physician."

Now, years later, I feel extremely fulfilled and needed, even after the last child left the nest. Linnie never makes a decision without asking my opinion, and we discuss any problems that arise together and reach a decision. He never "belittles" my problems and values my opinions and judgements. We work together, along with God, in this job of making a happy home. I still have my "bad days" and so does Linnie. But, praise the Lord, we have both learned to talk out our gripes and be completely honest with each other. In doing this, the problem is out in the open where we can both see it and deal with it with God's help and His will.

Chapter 21

MIRROR, MIRROR

It is very troubling to me the casual attitude many couples have when entering into marriage. "Well, if it doesn't work, so what? Divorce isn't so bad. We'll at least learn something from the experience."

I agree that experience is the best teacher. But marriage is for keeps. If you don't believe me, read the Bible.

I was not a victim of divorce, but I did emerge from my first marriage with a multitude of blunders, wrong decisions, and regrets. When I entered into my second marriage after the death of my husband, I determined to use those experiences to help me be the kind of wife and mother God wanted me to be.

One of my main problems was nagging. Looking back, I wonder how my husband survived so many caustic remarks about insignificant issues. At the time I thought HE was impatient, impetuous, and inconsiderate. But now I can see the real issue was – ME! My first marriage (which I entered into at the immature age of eighteen) was not founded on God's design for a union between man and wife. As a result, we experienced many days and nights of discord. It was only after I suffered the loss of my husband that I began to realize where and how I had failed my husband, Ed, myself, and God.

I used to complain constantly about the way Ed left our bathroom in disarray. I like for things to be neat and tidy. Most days I would find clothes on the floor, whiskers peppering the sink, toiletries left on the vanity, and the toilet left...well, you know what typically happens there. After Ed would read the newspaper, there would be sections scattered throughout the house. His clothes were left right where he dropped them every single day. I began to question |Ed's every move, and it wasn't a pretty sight. I did not take my complaints to God and ask for His guidance. I did not pray for God to help me stop complaining and show Ed more grace. And I did not ask God to bless my husband every day. Or thank God for giving me Ed. The seeds of resentment grew until they came dangerously close to choking the life out of our marriage.

It was my constant prayer after deciding to marry a second time that God would remove the awful habit of nagging from my personality. Or that I would seek God's face in this area. To be more tolerant when I needed to be and soften my spirit. Linnie and I talked about this many times before our marriage. "If you ever start to nag, I'll remind you," he reassured me. Since we both had already committed our new marriage to God, half the battle was won. God never fails, and He wondrously cured me of this awful sin. It was another of His miracles. I stand in awe today of the transformation.

I wanted to make my second marriage and home a place of peace and security. I wanted to hear God's voice, and be a Godly wife in every area of life. I began to read more and more of God's Word, especially Paul's instructions regarding the home and family, and my role in our family unit. Ephesians 5: 22-31 says,

> *"Wives, submit to your own husbands, as to the Lord. For the husband is head of the wife, as also Christ is head of the church; and He is the Savior of the body. Therefore, just as the church is subject to Christ, so let the wives be to their own husbands in everything. Husbands, love your wives, just as Christ also loved the church and gave Himself for her, that He might sanctify and cleanse her with the washing of water by the word, that He might present her to Himself a glorious church, not having spot or wrinkle or*

any such thing, but that she should be holy and without blemish. So husbands ought to love their own wives as their own bodies; he who loves his wife loves himself. For no one ever hated his own flesh, but nourishes and cherishes it, just as the Lord does the church. For we are members of His body, of His flesh and of His bones. "For this reason a man shall leave his father and mother and be joined to his wife, and the two shall become one flesh."

The entire message of the Christian life is one of submission. Paul talks to the wives first in his instructions and then to the husbands. Wives are afraid of submission because they sometimes believe it means oppression and total domination. On the contrary, Jesus yielded to God and in the same way He is asking wives to yield to their husbands. This is a voluntary submission by the wife to her husband's leadership. It does not mean that she is less important than her husband. What it does mean is that the wife reverences and respects her husband and yields to his decisions and directions. This command from the Bible does not mean that she is less important or weaker. "Agape love" toward another implies strength.

I believe this scripture in no way implies that man has the authority to mistreat or belittle his wife in any way. Rather, a man is to love his wife sacrificially and honor her. Just as Christ loves the church. A husband is to show "agape love" to his wife. When a husband and wife display this kind of love, each person in the marriage covenant will want the best for the other partner. Much of a husband's thoughts and activities should parallel the interests of his wife. Remember, they "become one" in the marriage commitment. Of course, men and women have different interests and tastes. And I'm not advocating that husbands and wives do everything together. But, when a husband loves his wife, as Christ loves the church, then he will often deny himself, and find that he truly desires what his wife does. The beauty of this is that the wife will acquire interests and likes similar to her mate. When the husband realizes these truths and practices them daily, then his wife will be more inclined to have a spirit of submission. The key to a successful, Christian marriage is to acknowledge God's headship. Then, the man seeks God's direction and the wife abides in the home under her husband's leadership. After this, the children are to be submissive to their parents. The children are told in the next verses *"Children, obey your parents in the Lord, for this is right. Honor your father and your mother, for this is the first commandment with a promise. (Eph. 6:1-2)*

So, you see, this picture of the relationships in a truly Christ-centered marriage in a beautiful way mirrors the relationship between Christ and His church.

Linnie makes all major decisions, (He always asks my opinion, but the final decisions are his.) and the children knew they had to approach him with any special requests. I am incredibly blessed in that Linnie always seeks God's will and direction, and God has beautifully honored this arrangement. I recommend it to all couples. This is God's ideal, and if you abide by it, your home will be richly blessed. I promise you.

From these instructions I learned the principles that I live by today - - the husband is the head of the home and should be given his rightful place - - in decisions, money managing, discipline, and any other area of the home. From the beginning I encouraged this principle, and God helped me have a submissive spirit to Linnie's leadership. Such a stark contrast to my rebellious attitude throughout my marriage to Ed.

I also made the mistake of not dedicating myself to my husband and his needs. I realized that a wife's basic function is to meet the needs of her husband. I can't remember many times when I put my husband's needs ahead of my own. Not wanting this mistake to recur, I began to read all I could find on marriage and the role of a godly wife. It became clear to me that my primary function as Linnie's wife was to be what he needed at any given time - -a listening ear, a lover, someone to complain to or a friend to be sad with. I determined to be that kind of wife, and it's been successful. I didn't say "easy", I said successful. It is only with God's daily help and strength that a marriage can really be a success anyway. Both Linnie and I still have "bad days" and sometimes I fall short of my responsibility of being a good wife. Sometimes we both have a "bad day" at the same time, and that really calls for patience and prayer!

A common failure of many couples is letting romance slip out of the marriage. Romance and sex are two separate things (I address this in detail in another chapter). I was no exception to this failure and as children came, I became so involved in caring for them and so tired after meeting their needs all day that I began to let myself and my job as a marriage partner go. I've had women tell me it's hard to be sexy after chasing kids all day, cleaning the house, doing the laundry, and "putting up with my husband's gripes about his day." And at the same time they complain that their husbands don't treat them as they did during courtship. Well, it is hard sometimes to be romantic in the middle of formulas, diapers, demanding teenagers, etc. Most women with small children are simply exhausted at night. But believe me, it's worth the effort to meet the physical needs of your husband. I feel like I need to state this again in **bold** print. **Find a way to meet the physical needs of your husband.**

Romance is putting a romantic note in your husband's lunch box. When Linnie and I married, I made a silent vow to keep the fire of romance burning in our lives, and it worked! Linnie was on shift work when we married. When he was on the 12-8 shift I would be at work when he arrived home. I sometimes left him a loving note on his pillow and sometimes left a note scotch taped to the mirror in our bathroom. When he was on 8-4 shift, I would slip a love note inside the wrapping on his sandwich. And I always got a call at work from him, telling me how much he loved me. This is romance! I guarantee you that if you begin a similar practice, you will reap many benefits! Even as I write this and after 46 years of marriage, Linnie seizes 1pportunities to be romantic. Right after rising, we both reach over to pull the covers up and make our bed.

Just the other morning, he looked over at me (Remember, this is with bedhair and no makeup!) and said, "How in the world can you be so beautiful first thing in the morning?" I can tell you that his comment makes up for any harsh words he might have spoken that didn't sit so well!

I bring Linnie his bedroom shoes at night when he's sitting in the den. I bring him coffee and a snack at night, and try to continually find ways to serve Linnie, to make him feel like a king. I realize that the majority of wives are working moms, and busy until bedtime. But every now and then think of ways to make your spouse feel loved, special, and remembered. Linnie always loved flowers, and I never knew when a delivery person would seek me out at work to bring me a huge bouquet from him with a love note attached. I'm sure he learned a thing or two from his first marriage union, too! You may not want to write notes, and giving compliments might be awkward for you at first. The point is to find a way to serve your husband. Even if you're tired. Even when you may not feel like it. Ladies, when you do, you will begin to be the queen of your home.

I never had patience before I married Linnie. Ever since I can remember, I was impatient when something didn't work right the first time I attempted it. I can vividly remember on many occasions in the past when I sewed and the garment didn't fit right or the zipper wasn't sewn in correctly, I would either discard it completely or give up on attempts to finish the project. I have always been impatient with people in general, with myself, and especially impatient in my handling of our son, Mark.

One of the few things I did not recognize in Linnie before our marriage was - - yes, you guessed it - - impatience. When I began to notice this several weeks after we moved into our home, I wondered how we would handle the problem. Linnie was worse than I, losing his patience very easily if something went amiss. I prayed daily about it, knowing we could get into terrific arguments if both of us had a tendency to react with anger or irritability. First of all, I asked God to grant me a "thick skin" every time Linnie lost patience with me or the children. I asked patience of God, patience to make up for Linnie's impatience, and patience to deal with the many problems that were sure to come in the coming months. And patience He gave me, as I was to discover day by day. Today, Linnie can still get impatient with people who are not walking with Christ, and he still gets impatient with me. But most times I just remain silent and ignore his edginess. I have learned over the years to respond and not react. And sometimes the response is to be silent.

In retrospect I can say that my prayer was answered as God moved in amazing ways. I found myself calming Linnie when he got upset over the fact that two cars wouldn't crank on a ten degree morning. When both of us had to go to work! Or simply when he couldn't find a tool. Or maybe when the children were too loud.

There were days when Mark would exasperate me with endless questions and demands. But instead of retaliating with screams and threats as in the past, I calmly reminded him that he had to consider other people and give me time to respond to his requests. This helped Mark tremendously in dealing with his own impatience. Every time I saw him getting upset, I would remind him lovingly to try again. Being a perfectionist, he would always get very angry if a project wasn't working out and tear it up in a fit of irritation. Over the years I have watched him deal with this problem and with much effort he has shown tremendous progress. Today, Mark is incredibly understanding with his son, and shows such tenderness towards others that it brings tears to my eyes!

Trying to get along with people, all kinds of people, is not an easy task, especially for children. When beginning our adventure, all of us needed a course in patience. It was more difficult for some than it was for others, to have tolerance with each other and patience with Linnie and me. Linnie had to learn to be longsuffering with Mark while I practiced extra understanding with some of his kids. I never tried to drastically change any of the children because I realized that they each had unique traits which I accepted. However,

I wanted to instill in them the golden rule - - whatever you wish that others would do to you, do also to them. (Matthew 7: 12)

Each morning I would start with a special prayer - - "God, I'm going to try, just for today, to be patient in all situations. If I slip, you just give me a nudge and remind me." At night I'd thank Him for getting me through that day. As the days moved into weeks, my patience <u>was</u> being cultivated as the children noticed a change. I'm not going to say it was smooth sailing, because it wasn't. The battle was up-hill many times. If you don't believe me, try living with nine other people and see. But God carried me day by day and He did "give me that nudge" many times when I fell short.

You know, children learn what they see. If they see hate, they will learn hatred. If they see love, they will learn charity and compassion. If they see generosity, they will learn that it is truly more blessed to give than to receive. In like manner, if they see impatience and anger, they will learn impatience and grow into selfish, self-centered adults. If they see God in their parents, they will seek God for themselves.

The attribute called "patience" is not easily attained, and learning to walk as children of God continues our whole life. There is only one way. To practice it daily so that our children can see it working out in our lives. And that is through a close walk with Jesus Christ. He is the only way that can make it possible for our weaknesses to be changed into strengths. Whenever I feel that I'm failing and just get "tired" of the struggle, I remember the words of Paul, *"I can do all things through Christ who strengthens me."* (Philippians 4:13)

Chapter 22

An Excellent Wife

"An excellent wife, who can find? Her worth is far above jewels . . She extends her hand to the poor, and she stretches out her hands to the needy . . Her children rise up and call her blessed, and her husband praises her . . She rises while it is still night and gives food to her household . . ."
(Proverbs 31)

I learned so many life lessons in my first marriage and was determined not to repeat them when I married the second time. I wanted very badly to be a Proverbs 31 woman and made a commitment to that end when Linnie and I married. There were many areas of my life which needed to be altered, and I immediately set about allowing the Holy Spirit to change my life and my personality.

The first thing I did was to make a list of my faults and shortcomings. High on that list was the tendency to be a nagging wife. I had a habit of nagging when I asked my husband to do something for me and and it wasn't done in a reasonable amount of time. This sometimes got results and sometimes it didn't. I knew it was very irritating at the time for him to be bothered constantly by an annoying and pestering wife. But I sure didn't stop. It says in Proverbs 21:19 *"It is better to live in a desert land than with a contentious* and vexing woman." and in Proverbs 27:15, *"A constant dripping on a day of steady rain and a contentious woman are alike"*. I must have sounded like a torrential downpour! It became a priority in my life to entreat the Holy Spirit to take over this area of my life. The progress in this was not an overnight change, but little by little I learned good behavior in this area.

Another area I tackled was my anger. Admittedly, I've thrown things in anger and frustration. Especially during my first marriage. But I haven't lost control in over forty years. So, what brought about the change in me? It was God. I sought help from the Holy Spirit, and have experienced victory over an area that at one time caused me and my family turmoil. But what a peace that covers me now! And I still get angry on occasion. I say angry, but it's really more of a feeling of frustration. Like when Linnie talks harshly to me or when I see followers of Christ making ungodly choices.

The Bible tells us that Jesus displayed anger and frustration when the money changers in the Temple were exploiting those who had come to worship. In the same light, most of the time I feel righteous indignation over the persecution of Christians in other countries, how the media expels most references to Christ, and disregards God's hand in anything that happens. Our country is widely turning away from Christ, and this causes me much exasperation. Jesus always loved the sinner, but hated the sin. And we should do the same. God expects believers to take a stand on Christian principles, with love and determination.

Another area I began to work on in my new marriage was complimenting my husband. I believe that any man "feeds on" compliments from his wife. I began to look for times in our daily lives that I could grace my husband with compliments, i.e., how good he looks in his Sunday suit and tie and how handsome he is on any day of the week. Whenever Linnie tackles a difficult job in our home, I always thank him and tell him what a good job he did. A valued husband feels respected, and a respected man has one of his deepest needs met. I never lose an opportunity to tell him that he is a good husband to me and father to our children. I also thank God daily for sending Linnie into my life forty-six years ago.

I believe a Proverbs 31 wife is a wife who stays busy in her home. Binge watching television programs even when they might be entertaining, is just a mindless addiction. And for what? When I made the decision that our children's television viewing would be limited, our lives took on a new meaning. I was always available to help one or more of the kids with homework at night, and when I did have some spare time, crocheting re-entered my life. I began to seek out Christian authors and reading became a hobby for me. I spent time in the kitchen cooking meals I knew the family would enjoy, and made lots of homemade cookies. Whether you make homemade or store bought cookies, it doesn't matter. To be up and working in the home is good for the mind, body, and spirit. And it makes the home special, a place of refuge and rest. Many times Linnie and I would enter into a game of Twister or Monopoly with the children. Or some of them may have needed my help in baking a batch of cookies. It took time, and it required my involvement.

In 1976 I began to look at my life as wife and mother of eight children and found myself sorely lacking. In my prayer life, I began to feel that God was telling me to quit work. I told Him that was impossible with four children in college. My job was a very fulfilling one which I hated to leave. I began having headaches and many nights I would be awake at 2:30 a.m., unable to sleep. I continued to hear God telling me, "I will provide for you." But I kept ignoring Him. Linnie was concerned about my health, and he told me one day, "Sweetheart, we can make it with God's help. I don't know how we will, but we will. If He is telling you to give up your job, then do it."

Then the stomach problems began, and eating was practically impossible for me. I missed a considerable amount of work because of my condition. Many days I was doubled over in pain, with nausea and intense agony. One day I took the day off and drove to Orangeburg to visit a friend of mine, Pastor Lynn Corbett. I cried while we talked that day, and I'll always remember this nugget of advice that he gave me. He said, "Annette, if you hear God's call on your life and ignore that call, you are going to have a miserable life." On my way back to Norway, I began to cry out to the Lord and told Him, "Okay, God, I give it all to you, my husband, my children, my life, and my job. Do with them and me as you wish, but I need your peace!" I didn't get an immediate answer from heaven, but when I got home, I typed out my resignation to be turned in the following morning at work.

That night, I slept through the night for the first time in months. My stomach problem ceased that night, and I felt complete peace and contentment. And God did provide, because all four of those in college got through it by loans, grants, and much prayer. Also, our last four children put themselves through in the same way. That's the way a Proverbs 31 wife would do it- -finally giving it to the Lord.

One goal in my marriage was that Linnie would "rise up and praise me, and call me blessed." After I resigned my job, most of my time was devoted to my children and their needs and the needs of Linnie. I began during that time to send encouragement cards to the sick and those who needed to be touched by prayer. It was wonderful to be available when the kids arrived home from school, and they could share with me about their day before study time. The four kids at home had it a lot easier than the older ones because I was there to do the laundry and help with supper. I still required the children to do their chores, but there was more time for me to just be there as their mom. I was always aware of how Linnie viewed me, how he saw me as a wife, mother, and keeper of our household. But he always had affirming words for me in our home.

Not long after I gave up my job, Linnie's mom developed colon cancer and severe respiratory problems. We took her into our home as her condition worsened. She was in a wheel chair for a while until she became bed-ridden. She talked often of heaven and how she saw her mom on several occasions. She and I always talked about when God would call us to heaven, what a glorious day that would be.

She spent her last Christmas with us when all of the kids gathered at our home. Cindy brought her guitar and played for us. It was a real "God moment" in her bedroom as the children drifted in and out, singing hymns and carols to her. The light was dim in the room, and you could feel the presence of the Holy Spirit in our midst. One night toward the end of her earthly life I was sitting with her while Linnie got his shower. She hadn't spoken for about three days, but I continued to talk to her like she could hear me. When Linnie relieved me so that I could get my shower, I said to her, "Grandma, I'm going to take my shower now. Don't you die while I'm gone, you hear me?" She suddenly opened her eyes and said, "Well, if I do, I'd want you to be clean!" She never spoke again after that brief statement. I always felt that it was a great honor to share those last months with a very wise and gracious lady.

About five years after Grandma Sutcliffe passed away, my own mother, Susie Brunson, had congestive heart failure. She also experienced two heart attacks while in her own home. The story is often shared that she drove herself to the emergency room while in the throes of a heart attack. A guard met Mom at the entrance and said, "Sorry, Ma'am, you can't park here." She looked at him and said, "I'm parking here. Sir, I'm having a heart attack." Mom then handed him her keys! During another attack, after calling 911, Mom flagged the ambulance driver at the highway to take her to the hospital. Where my mom lacked tactfulness, she sure had grit. She moved into our home as her health needs progressed. Linnie and I ministered to her throughout her bouts with congestive heart failure. My mom could be very direct, and many times I had to check myself to keep from answering her in like manner. But I would remind myself that I was trying to be a Proverbs 31 woman. I tried to always talk to my mom in a soft tone. Her life ended in a perfect way, sitting in her favorite chair, crocheting and holding a glass of water! I was thankful to open our home to both of our aging mothers. What an honor and a privilege!

After my decision to leave work, I began a jail ministry. I visited once a week and ministered to the prisoners, both male and female. We had Bible study and I also sang for them. Cindy accompanied me several times and brought her guitar to lead worship in the prison. She also sang a few solos during our meetings. I thoroughly enjoyed these times when I could share my testimony and pray with the prisoners. It felt extremely strange hearing the heavy iron gate snapping shut behind me when I entered. Rising breakouts and prison tensions ended my ministry there after two years.

Here am I, forty-six years later, still trying to serve others in my quest to be a Proverbs 31 woman. To rise up early, to meet the ever changing needs of my family, to seek God daily, and be a woman of noble character. I fail many times, but it is a constant joy meeting my husband's needs and the needs of others. But it is a true sense of contentment when I do succeed. Why don't you try it?

Chapter 23

ACCEPT, ADAPT, LOVE

M any women who enter the lifetime commitment of marriage do not realize what a sacred commitment it is – nor do they realize the tremendous sacrifices they must make for their husbands and families. But boy it's worth it. And the rewards are truly great.

To accept someone fully, as is necessary in a marriage partnership, is a tall order. Accepting means overlooking, forgetting, and ignoring. It means not mentioning obvious faults. It means not putting your man down. It means never comparing him with someone else. Accepting means concentrating on the good points of your man and miraculously the bad points will melt away. After all, if you won't accept his faults, who will? A man needs to feel accepted and respected. It's a basic need, just as a woman longs to feel needed.

I determined before I walked down the isle to accept Linnie, hang-ups and all, his faults, shortcomings and irritating habits. And I was sure he had them, though I hadn't noticed any before we got married. Seldom, during courtship, does a couple see each other's faults. The old saying, "You have to live with somebody twenty-four hours a day to really know him" is definitely true. This must be another one of God's miracles. If we could see all the faults of each other while courting, some would never make it to the altar.

A man needs to be accepted as he is, just exactly as he is. This total acceptance shows him in a marvelous way how much you really love him, - - and love begets love. Total acceptance will make him adore you and that adoration will begin to spill over into all the areas of your life together. A man needs a friend as well as a wife, lover, and homemaker - - a friend who'll accept him unconditionally. It makes him feel free. This kind of accepting love in the Bible is called "agape" love. It is the same kind of love that God has for us, His children.

I knew if I didn't accept Linnie totally, exactly as he was, I'd nag him, and that was my greatest fear. I've always been a nag by nature. I didn't want to be or mean to be, but I just was. My children can all attest to my nagging nature since it still "shows itself" at times. I knew if I began nagging Linnie, he would probably withdraw, stop communicating, and feel caged, hemmed in, instead of free. So many wives needlessly nag their husbands right out the door, oftentimes right into another woman's arms - - someone who <u>will</u> accept him. At least for a short period of time.

I still slip occasionally - - my old sinful nature keeps me from being perfect. But when I do slip, either God or Linnie will gently remind me that I need to do some self-examination. Then I begin anew, trying harder than before to be a better wife and friend to my husband.

I'm sure that my faults were clouded from Linnie's view by the newness of love and the fact that we didn't have much time to be together. We both had our families and careers during courtship that demanded much of our time. The time we spent together was so cherished we never thought about flaws. Everything seemed so right and so perfect, and Linnie seemed to be "the ideal man." Having been through one marriage, the adjustments, traumas, and moments of soul-searching that came the first year didn't throw me as badly as they do many women.

The idea that marriage is "50-50" is simply not true. That may be a shock to some, but I'm sure that even many men will agree that most of the adapting, changing, and adjusting is done by the woman if the marriage is to be successful. God gave man the greater capacity to be strong leaders, but to woman he gave the stronger ability to accept, adapt, and adjust in any situation. It is when she refuses to use this ability that a woman fails in a marriage relationship. When Linnie and I married and I moved to Norway, my three kids and I had a tremendous adjustment. We had to change to a new home, a new town, and a new school. If a woman expects her mate to adapt or conform to her dream of what she wants him to be, she fights a losing battle from the start. After all, she didn't fall in love with a dream. She fell in love with a man, a human being with all the frailties and imperfections that go along with being human.

Marriages are "made in heaven", but we have to work them out here on earth! God created and established the home and family, but imperfect, sinful human beings have the responsibility of working at the relationship daily with determination to make it work. The greater portion of this responsibility rests with the woman, for she is created with an enormous capacity to change and adapt. Dads have an imposing task to cope with the many emotional changes that occur in our children from birth to adulthood. It's hard enough for a momma! An outburst of crying from one of our adolescents would throw Linnie off for several hours. He just didn't know how to process or handle it. But a woman has a built-in capacity to adjust to new situations, however drastic or minute they might be. It is her gift to be able to handle with care the unending needs of young children, teens who suddenly can't cope with this thing called "growing up", to many times multi-task and to manage the ever changing needs of a family.

I began the new challenge of a second marriage well aware that my husband, Linnie, hadn't received "divine immunity" from having faults. One of the first things I detected to be a possible source of trouble for me was Linnie's impatience - - with himself, the kids and sometimes even me. If he was working on a project and it went haywire, he became irritable with whoever was closest to him. If he wasn't feeling well or beset with problems at work, I learned quickly that "silence was golden." At first I found myself gently rebuking him for being out of sorts, chastising him for his attitude. Suddenly one day it dawned on me that his biting tone or impatient attitude when things went amiss were an integral part of his personality. Was it fair to try to change him, to remake him into something I felt was better? So, I set about to accept this part of his personality. And I slowly began a practice of thanking God for the part of his personality I found hard to accept. At the same time God was working through me by granting me patience and understanding to cope with any fault that I might discover in Linnie.

Linnie is a gruff speaker. It's his nature - the way God made him. He doesn't know how to talk softly and when he speaks, it sounds more like a small yell. For the first year of our marriage I nursed hurt feelings many times. He would speak to one of the kids and I would say, "Well, you don't have to yell." "I am <u>not</u> yelling", was his reply, or I would ask him a question and he would reply in what I considered a harsh tone. "Don't get so upset", I'd say. "I'm not upset - - this is the way I talk." We went on like this until I came to the point of admitting to myself that Linnie was never going to be soft-spoken or tender in his speech because he wasn't made that way. I knew this could be a source of real trouble in our marriage if I didn't learn to cope with it. It was already causing a little friction between us. But I decided with prayer to accept it, deal with my own feelings, and it ceased to be a source of irritation to me. I wanted to accept this part of Linnie's personality, but in my own strength I could never have done it. I turned it over to the Holy Spirit, and He dealt with my feelings and made it easier for me. He worked through me to not only accept Linnie as he was, but also to be an example to my three kids who were having the same problem that I was having. After that, if Mark complained, "Why does Daddy yell so much?" I could say, "Yes, he responds harshly sometimes and even yells some. That doesn't mean he loves you any less. He talks loud to me sometimes, too. That's the way he is, and we all have to accept it."

One of the hardest things I wrestled with during our first year was Linnie's shyness about his relationship with Christ. I've always been very open and vocal about my love for and devotion to Jesus. I believed that Linnie was a born-again believer, but after we got married I began to notice that he never discussed this relationship openly in our home. He was very quick to point out to the children their responsibility as followers of Christ and would never begin a meal without returning thanks to God. He taught Sunday school regularly and always read his Bible before going to bed. But doubts began to creep into my mind concerning his faith and commitment to Christ, wondering at times if he wasn't a little pharisaic in his faith. As I wrestled with this, I tried to subtly pick him for answers to my queries. It was only after reading a marvelous book, "Fascinating Womanhood", that I felt more secure. The author states that some people have a very private faith and relationship to Christ. And that a woman should never expect a man, if he's not wired to be expressive, to talk openly about faith matters. I'm convinced that God led me to that book because I was finally able to understand and accept this difference in our personalities.

Later, I found out in conversations with Linnie that he had stood his ground as a believer at work among lost co-workers who would ridicule his faith. I believe God began to move in Linnie's life, too, as I committed this problem to Him. Slowly Linnie was more open and vocal about his commitment to Christ. Not long after that Linnie began farming a portion of land to help with college expenses for the kids. Together, we dedicated the farm to God because He had blessed us so abundantly. I have witnessed my husband become more open about God's hand in our lives, and we now discuss our relationship with Jesus openly and marvel at the many miracles God performs in our lives.

This thing of acceptance works two ways and I knew Linnie would find areas of my personality that were difficult for him to live with. I tried to warn him before our marriage about my obvious faults, but he kept insisting I had none. (Oh, the blindness of new love!) I knew I was extremely "thrifty" (my friends call it tight) sometimes to the point of raving about the cost of an item.

Very early in our marriage we bought a riding lawn mower for our large yard. Well, needless to say, everyone wanted to mow the grass even if it didn't need to be cut. One afternoon Linnie came in from the yard and said he had been riding around on the mower. Before I put my mind in gear, I put my mouth in motion. "My goodness, we sure can't afford gas for you to pleasure ride around the yard." Linnie just shook his head as he washed his hands, not saying a word. I could have cut my tongue out, but it was too late! James said,". . But the tongue can no man tame, it is an unruly evil, full of deadly poison." (James 3:8) Isn't that true? I just have to ask God to tame my tongue every single day. Set a guard, oh Lord, over my mouth, keep watch over the door of my lips. (Psalm 141:3) And it sure is hard for a woman to do!

I praise the Lord daily for Linnie's tolerance and understanding because he never once rebuked me or became angry. I've been guilty of making comments like "You shouldn't have spent so much on that gift", the time he gave me a love beaded necklace - or the time he sent me a dozen long stemmed, red roses for our anniversary. And then when he got home I greeted him with "Thank you, sweetheart, but you shouldn't have, they cost too much!" God opened my eyes to the folly of my obsession with expenses. Being "tight" remains a part of my personality and probably always will. It is my nature to stretch a dollar as far as it will go and look for bargains every time I shop. It was always a challenge when we had ten to feed to keep the grocery bill down by taking one chicken and making three casseroles to feed twelve people. (Linnie asked me one night where the chicken was in the chicken-rice casserole. He said he saw plenty of rice but couldn't find the chicken!) The wonder of it was the way he accepted this personality trait of mine and never tried to remold me. I've learned a lot with the Holy Spirit as my teacher and guide.

When I receive a gift from Linnie or flowers (which he still loves to send) I gratefully accept them in love, put an imaginary bridle on my tongue, and let him worry about the cost.

I still have my quirks, and so does Linnie. We still "bug" each other at times. But we've both learned to accept each other and God has given us both the ability to overlook the faults of each other in the process. The marvelous part is when you accept each other unconditionally, as God accepts us, utilizing "agape love, the faults don't bother you nearly as much. Ours is truly a marriage made in heaven. Yours can be, too.

Submission – Easy Word, Tougher Job

Submission - - an easy enough word to pronounce, easy enough to spell, but what does it have to do with two people entering a marriage covenant? In today's world of "Equal Rights", "Total Equality", etc., how can this word fit into a marriage? In many marriages it doesn't, but in ours submission is one of the keys to our success.

The first year was the toughest for Linnie and me, as is true for most couples. There were so many adjustments for us, magnified many times because of the number of people involved in the marriage. For me the battle was doubly hard because this thing of submission wasn't coming easy for me. I had accepted God's will for me to place myself under the authority of my husband, but it's easier said than done. Without God's constant encouragement it would be impossible, especially in today's society where we get "SEXUAL EQUALITY" hurled at us from all sides.

I began to feel a certain amount of relief in taking problems to Linnie for his decision. It left me free to tackle the multitude of household tasks and minor problems that came up each day. And the miracle of it was that Linnie never made a decision without asking my advice. When Polly wanted special permission to attend a party with a date before her 16th birthday, I took her request to

Linnie. But he didn't make a decision without asking, "What do you think?" Sometimes he takes my advice, sometimes he weighs it and makes a decision against my advice, but I accept the decision as final and honor it as his wife. Sometimes I didn't agree with his decisions but, after stating my objections, I accepted them and so did the kids. One of our girls began dating the same boy every week. She still had two more years of school, and neither Linnie nor I wanted her to get too involved with one boy. We only allowed the girls to date once a week, and he made the decision that if they dated one boy steadily, they could only date every other week. I thought this was a bit harsh, giving them only two dates a month, but I understood his reasons and accepted his decision. The girls were disappointed, I am sure, but they were not bitter nor resentful, and they accepted his reasons for the rule. We were criticized by some people for being so strict on the children. However, Linnie said these weren't their kids, and we were raising them God's way. Some women say, "I couldn't live that way", or, "No man will tell me what to do." Well, if you expect to have a happy, secure marriage, girls, learn to submit. It really is God's ideal for the home.

Our kids always knew that God was the head of our home. That Daddy was under God's authority, Mom submitted to Dad's decisions, and the children were subject to us both. They have always respected that line of authority and I hope they have carried this into their own marriages.

In counseling one couple I stressed this important basis for marriage. Entering into a new marriage relationship using God's formula for the home, gives husband, wife, and the family a firm foundation. If a man is stripped of his place of honor, if his authority is taken from him, the home will not rest on God's ordained plan. I know of one couple, married over twenty years, who are "living together", but not happy. For twenty years the wife made all major decisions concerning the children, finances, even where they would go on vacation. And where was the husband? He simply lived in the home, and worked to provide the things his wife and children wanted to buy. How miserable. How unfulfilling. The children didn't seem to respect either parent because even they knew something was wrong with the family dynamics.

I realize that it may seem a strange way to operate a home, but it works. Remember, this formula for authority in the home is God's plan, not mine. Some may say, "It isn't fair - - why do I have to submit? Why not the man, at least some of the time?" Because God ordained the institution of marriage and He gave the rules. If His rules are applied, the marriage will stand the test of time. If God's principles are ignored, conflicts that arise between husband and wife may drive deep, dividing wedges leaving the children confused and hurt in the process.

I am not saying that a wife is inferior to her husband - - rather that she must be under her husband's authority and leadership if the marriage is to succeed. When a wife submits, she simply solves the problem of two selfish, sinful people colliding head-on in a marriage relationship.

I have a friend whose husband is also head of the home – but in a different way. He controls all the finances and handles all matters relating to the home without consulting his wife. She isn't allowed the privilege of writing a check. She told me one day that she had no idea how much her husband made and the only way she got any new clothes was to "pad" the grocery bill for extra money. This is not God's ideal for marriage and the home. The husband is head of his home, but he fails to heed Paul's advice to "Love your wife as yourself". Then problems will surely arise.

In many marriages, the wife rules. In some homes there are two trying to rule, with constant clashes of opinion and who should win out. Neither of these arrangements can work, either, because God ordained man to be at the head of the home and man is equipped for that responsibility.

A man wants a woman with opinions, and she should be able to express her opinions with dignity. And then support her husband's final decision whether it clashes with her opinion or not. Wow!

That's a tall order isn't it? I found it very hard at first to accept Linnie's decisions as final when I disagreed with him. When I tell him "It's your decision. Whatever you decide I'll support you", I find that he earnestly seeks my opinion and weighs his decisions carefully. He knows that I do stand behind him in all decisions. Linnie treats me like a queen, not because of any special ability I may have, but because I give him the honor of being "King of his home."

This thing of submission includes a certain amount of adapting -- adapting to his way of life, his friends, his hobbies, etc. I remember making the statement before Linnie and I were married, "I'd never make a farmer's wife. I hate farming, chickens, cows, and anything else connected with farming." Well, about three years later we were farming sixty-five acres in addition to Linnie working full time. We planted and gathered our own vegetables, planted and harvested hay, and he wanted to get some chickens to give the younger children a little extra responsibility in addition to giving us our own egg supply. (We sometimes used 5-6 dozen eggs a week.) I can't say it was easy adapting to Linnie's love for the ground. Many times when we were first married I found myself balking at any idea of his farming endeavors. I wanted no part of cows, chickens, or pigs. I fussed about the dirt he tracked into the house from the fields.

I remember one night not long after we were married, I noticed Linnie doing some figuring. When I asked what he was doing, he said, "I've been trying to calculate whether it would pay to buy about fifteen calves, raise them, and sell them next spring." I quickly said, "Oh, you'll never make money that way. They're too much trouble anyway." I could see the disappointment in his face and he never mentioned the proposal again. Later I asked him to forgive me and he did, but I carried that guilt for a long time. I had a lot to learn about being an ideal, submissive wife.

As the Holy Spirit began to move in my life, He opened my eyes to the hurt I must be causing Linnie by not adapting to his way of life. By crushing any plans he might mention about farming or ignoring them altogether, I was keeping him from functioning as he should in the home. He was also withdrawing within himself with his dream, and a barrier had begun to exist in our communication. So, I made up my mind that whatever Linnie liked, I would like. If he had a dream to farm, to own 50 cows or 50 chickens, that would be my dream too. Why? Because when we married, we became as one. I can't explain how my attitude about farming changed except to say the Holy Spirit began to fill my heart and life about two years after our marriage. As He controlled my life, my attitudes about everything and everybody took on a new dimension. I'm not saying it was an automatic happening. Sometimes I had to be "leaned on" by the Lord to adapt. But as I began to take an interest in Linnie's interests, my life was blessed - - and I learned so many new things.

I never thought I'd sit for hours while Linnie explained how a piece of farm machinery was put together - - or sit in a boat, quiet (which is a real struggle for me) for three hours fishing, with bugs, flies, and mosquitoes to keep me company. I really think the hardest thing I've done was sit and watch three football games on television in one afternoon when I have never been a football fan!

One afternoon Linnie came into the den where I was reading. He was ecstatic. "The garden seed just arrived", he exclaimed! Well, who can get excited over pea seed, corn seed, or okra seed? Linnie can! He was like a small boy as he took each package out of the box, explaining what each was. I could have ignored him and gone on with my reading. Three or four years ago, I would have. But I didn't. I put my book down and became engrossed in his excitement, sharing his joy as best I could. I asked him one day why he loved to plant so much, since he always planted more than we could possibly use. He answered, "Annette, I just love to watch the ground until it breaks open with new life, and then watch it grow from a tiny speck to a full plant, bearing fruit. It's just real special, watching that miracle every year." The excitement in his eyes convinced me that I had to share this love of his in order to really be a part of who he is. And share I have. Every summer we gather what God allows us to grow, shell the beans, cut the okra, and freeze or can what we glean.

I know of so many couples who take separate vacations because neither can agree on anything and they have such separate interests. So, they go their separate ways, unable to enjoy the closeness, the warmness of being together. One summer, Linnie and I had been trying to get away for a weekend. Well, my idea of a free weekend would be staying in a plush resort with room service, swimming pool, etc. (close to a shopping center, of course). I knew without asking that Linnie's idea of the weekend would be camping out on the lake in our fold-out camper and getting up at 5:00 a.m. (to catch the early ones!). I don't remember exactly where we went for that weekend, but as a submissive, adaptable wife, I'm sure I was ready with my bug spray, mosquito net, and fishing gear.

Sometimes Linnie makes it hard for me to adapt to him because so many times he wants to adapt to me. He is so kind, considerate, and thoughtful, whenever we plan to go somewhere he always says, "Where do you want to eat?" Then I say, "It doesn't matter to me." He asks again, "Where do you want to eat?" And I reply "It doesn't matter." "Yes it does." So, many times I choose the place he would prefer, simply because I want to please him. You see, it doesn't really matter where we go or what we do, as long as we're together.

A great challenge of marriage is to blend two sinful and selfish lives so completely that they go through life as one, despite the fact that they are two distinct personalities. Most of the time two vastly different personalities.

I've come a long way in all these years. But not in my own power. As I submitted to the Holy Spirit, I was molded into the kind of wife God intended me to be. And it has reaped great rewards. For it is only when a woman fully submits to her husband, worships and serves him daily, willingly, and lovingly that he recognizes her worth and beauty and praises her. Then she can become what she is intended to be - - a rare, priceless treasure to her man and the envy of many other women.

Chapter 24

A MARVELOUS MIRACLE

The Rev. Billy Graham said, "Sex is a gift from God—not only for the propagation of the race, but for enjoyment—only in the bonds of matrimony. Sex is a creative energy and can be a tremendous dynamo for good in life if directed in the right direction."

This is the central idea we have tried to instill in our children. There is such a great difference between "sex" and "love expressed through sex." This marvelous miracle, this creative energy, is truly a gift from God—a powerful gift which can be misused and abused if not controlled by Him. Sex without God's control lasts only a moment. With His control, it lasts for a lifetime. If we surrender our sexuality to Christ, practice sexual intimacy within the marital relationship, this gift can truly be a source of much pleasure and enjoyment. It took me many years to learn that every gift from God must be under His control if we are to be useful servants of His.

In our home sex was not a "hush" topic. I have always maintained an open mind regarding sex, and as the children matured I encouraged them to talk openly about any questions they had. I always answered questions directly as best I could without any embarrassment, and I have heard some complex questions!

A dear friend, who was also my family doctor, Dr. Ira B. Horton, helped me immensely. He said, "Annette, always talk easily with your children about sex, just as easily as you would about the weather or last night's ball game. If you do, they will always come to you for answers when they are curious about sex. Never let them feel embarrassed for having asked and never put them off until a more convenient time. Keep the lines of communication open. Present sex to them as a beautiful gift from God to be used and not abused." Those words of wisdom carried me through the adolescent years with our children.

I grew up in a time when sex just wasn't discussed within the family relationship. So much erroneous information was fed into the minds of young people because of the "silent" attitude of most parents. I vividly remember several times when my mother did talk with me about maturing, changes in the body, etc., I was extremely embarrassed and I think she was, too. What could have been some beautiful moments of sharing between mother and daughter were tense and awkward. That was the way it was fifty years ago. Today, we are living in a culture that has dropped almost all taboo and censorship in this vital area. Either side of this pendulum swing is dangerous. Somewhere, right down the broad middle of the road, there must be a place for open and frank discussion about sex, keeping in mind the beauty as well as the power of this wonderful gift.

At the outset of our marriage, I could tell that Linnie was not as "frank" about the topic of sex as I was. So, I set about to "condition" his outlook a bit before I shocked him too much. At first there were times when he squirmed in his chair, cleared his throat, or changed the subject, but as the months passed I noticed that some of his inhibitions were fading. Today we discuss anything and everything regarding sex without the slightest hesitation.

I could tell very early that my five new kids were not accustomed to such frankness, so I tread softly so I wouldn't offend any of them. As time passed, I noticed that they began to discuss very personal matters with me without embarrassment.

Sex education is vital to young people. It is as necessary as learning history or science. When a couple accepts parenthood, they should also accept the responsibility of educating their children about sex as well. It's as much a part of a child's life as instructions on tying shoes. Too many times parents leave sex education up to schools, their children's friends, or the media. In many cases this kind of enlightenment is distorted and a misconstrued conception of sex. How sad!

When our children began dating, I talked with each one, explaining that the privilege of dating also carried certain heavy responsibilities. The boys were admonished to treat every girl with respect and honor, an individual created by God in His likeness. Our girls were counseled on the importance of keeping their standards high, according to God's commands. If we belong to the King, then we must be loyal subjects. In 1 Corinthians 6:19-20, God says, *"Do you not know that your bodies are temples of the Holy Spirit, who is in you, whom you have received from God? You are not your own; you were bought at a price. Therefore honor God with your bodies"*. It took me many years in my early life to learn and live by that principle. It became paramount in our home that we address sexuality, educate our children according to God's word, and guide them as teenagers, especially when dating became a part of their lives. Parents, I implore you. Don't assume that your children know how to respond to sexual advances in the dating realm. Acknowledge the sexual aspect of dating, present your children with scenarios, and most importantly discuss with them possible ways to respond when temptations arise.

In today's culture our entertainment media is flooded with sex-oriented films and programs. Our young people desperately need a casual and frank approach to this vital subject—a Christian approach that emphasizes the beauty of this precious gift. Dr. Charlie Shedd, psychologist and author of "The Stork is Dead", relates to young people regarding every aspect of sexuality. It's a marvelous book, and every one of our teenagers read and enjoyed it. Give your growing teenagers godly based reading material about the subject of sex. If you don't, they will surely seek out the World

Wide Web's plethora of information. And as you can imagine, most of the world's message on sex is distorted, deceptive, and blatantly contrary to God's holy word.

As each of the children matured and began to be aware of their own distinct sexuality, I was careful to answer all questions honestly, always stressing the importance of God's place in their lives. Some of my more joyful moments have been spent talking with the kids about such topics as abortion, pre-marital sex, adultery, petting, etc. Cindy came up to me one day while I was busy in the kitchen preparing supper and asked, "Mom, how often do wives and husbands have sex?" Well, I was a little stunned for a second, but we had a nice discussion on the subject right there in the kitchen—while I fried chicken!

A normal sex drive is one of the most priceless gifts God has given us. When God created man and woman, He created sexuality and looked at it with approval saying, "It is very good." Sex isn't sin. But misusing it is. Dr. Charles Shedd also states that what young people call "all the way" isn't sex. It's not even one-fourth of the way or even an eighth of the way. Real sex means total involvement. He notes, "Sex at its greatest isn't free. It's for those who are willing to pay the price of total commitment."

Sex is a priceless gift from our Lord, to be used by two persons who are willing to commit to each other for LIFE in a marriage relationship. Sexual desires are a natural part of growing, maturing, and becoming adults. All of our children were encouraged to turn their sexuality over to Christ along with the other areas of their lives. Sex, a complex subject, and the most erroneously discussed topic of all times, yes. But, ahhh a marvelous miracle ordained by a magnificent, holy God!

EPILOGUE

Well! We have come to the end of our adventure together. The years have come and gone, and all eight of our children have grown, gone out, and made lives of their own. It is with a note of sadness that I end this journey! I've opened up our home and lives to you in hopes of reaching many young couples who are contemplating a life together. If I can reach just one couple with our story of life with Jesus as head of our home, I will consider this project a success.

We have traveled through the years, explored our many adjustments of embracing a blended family unit, and how we made it work with the help and guidance from God. The Holy Spirit was, and still is, the foundation of all we've accomplished in our family. He "held us together" during the hard times. I didn't want to leave you with the impression that "all was rosy". There were many joyous days, but also difficult moments in our family. Without Christ as our leader, I don't think we would have made it.

In the silent years of this book, I was chosen to be the Times and Democrat Region "Mother of the Year" in 2007 and "South Carolina 2010 Mother of the Year". I have been granted many opportunities to share with others some of the truths within these pages. Remember, wherever you find yourself in life, whatever your circumstances might be, you can reach out to others and "be the light God wants you to be". I am grateful for these opportunities because I have had a burden for young couples for many years.

Before I close, I am sure you may be curious about what our children are doing at the present time and how their lives have progressed. So, I will introduce you to them again, in order of their ages:

First, the oldest of our kids is Linnie, Jr., 63 years of age, still as handsome as he was in 1973 with distinguished grey sideburns. He graduated from Clemson University with a poultry science degree and a commission of 2nd Lieutenant in the Armed Services. He loves woodworking and has made several pieces of furniture. He retired from Boeing Electronics as a lead estimator, and he and his wife, Brenda, make their home in Bonney Lake, Washington.

Next in line is Thea, now 61. Thea is an avid reader. She graduated from Orangeburg-Calhoun Technical College with a degree in Laboratory Technology and has never deviated from that calling. Thea has always been fully dedicated to her profession and is now looking forward to retirement. She has a sunny personality that puts everyone at ease. We have grown closer over the years, and I always look forward to her visits. If I need help, all I have to do is give her a call and she is here in no time. She and her husband, Brad, have two sons and make their home in North, South Carolina.

Polly is 61, with long, brown hair. She is still my even-tempered child, always ready to calm others down if they get ruffled. She graduated from Orangeburg Regional Hospital School of Nursing as a registered nurse and worked until her first child was born. She and her husband, Rodney, have two children and one precocious grandchild. They live in Columbia, South Carolina. Polly began a thriving business, Lady Street Soaps, in 2012, and participates in markets throughout the state.

Close behind Polly is Eddie, now 60. Eddie is our computer genius and man of many talents. Eddie has had two careers. He graduated from Clemson University with a master's degree in Architecture, opened a business for many years, and then returned to the University of South Carolina and obtained a degree in Computer Engineering. He and his wife, Louie, have two children and one grandchild. Louie recently opened Tiger Lily Flower Farm, featuring fresh cut seasonal flowers and expertly designed bouquets. Louie sells flowers at local markets, and also contracts for fresh flower deliveries. Eddie designed their home, nestled in the woodlands of Little Mountain, South Carolina. He and Louie can be found most weekends working on intricate landscaping and new improvements to their beautiful yard and gardens. That is, if Clemson doesn't have a home football game!

Next to Eddie is Julie, 58 years of age. Julie is my organizer of social activities. If she hears of any event coming up, she can organize it to the last detail, telling all of the kids what to bring and where to congregate! Julie still enjoys arranging flowers, and has been the floral designer for several weddings. She is very devoted to us, calling several times a week. She will clean, cook, or do whatever we need when one of us is ailing. Julie, a LPN, works in a Columbia medical practice, and rarely if ever misses a day of work. She has a zealous work ethic, and is truly dedicated to her patients. She and her husband, Jay, make their home in Gaston, South Carolina.

Cindy is 57, with blonde hair and blue eyes. As a child, Cindy dreamed of recording songs to share her love for Christ. With the support and encouragement from her husband Chuck, she composed many songs and later recorded three musical projects. She continues to minister to a variety of audiences through Christian testimony and song. Cindy has struggled with migraine headaches since childhood and continually seeks God's grace to deal with chronic pain today. Cindy graduated from Winthrop College with a degree in early childhood education and worked for 32 years as a kindergarten teacher. She retired from teaching and recently launched her own business, KMA Jewelry Designs. Cindy and her husband, Chuck, have three children, one of whom has gone to make her home with the Lord. They also have two grandchildren and make their home in Cameron, South Carolina.

Mark, our youngest son, is now 55 years old. After graduation he enlisted in the Air Force. While in the service he excelled, earning bachelor and master degrees in Political Science. In his spare time, Mark enjoys singing and tweaking recordings with Pro Tools Audio equipment. He loves riding ATVs and meticulously engages in home projects. Mark is now working for the Defense Department in Washington. He has two children and makes his home in Virginia.

Our youngest, who doesn't like to be called "the baby" is Janet, 55 years of age. Janet has always loved the outdoors, preferring to work outside or join her dad for a day of fresh water fishing. She lives near us and is very protective of Linnie and me, checking on us several times a week or stopping by often to share a dish she has prepared. After graduation, Janet enlisted in the Air Force for a time. Janet joined the South Carolina Air National Guard and is a Senior Master Sergeant. Later in life, she graduated from Orangeburg-Calhoun Technical College with a degree in X-Ray Technology and works at a Pain Center in Orangeburg, South Carolina. Janet and her husband, Bracky, have two children and five grandchildren. They make their home in Norway, South Carolina.

Lastly, the patriarch of our family, is Linnie Sr., now eighty-seven years of age and still very active. He is truly the love of my life. He still grows a garden every spring and harvests the vegetables for me to freeze and can (with his help). We also can jams and jellies which we share with others. Do you recall earlier that I mentioned how Linnie wanted to add chickens to our menagerie of animals? And how I most certainly did not? Well, several years ago, our children all contributed to purchase a chicken coop for their dad. (with my blessing!) He now has chickens and spends many afternoons doting over his hens. He gathers eggs daily and gives away dozens to our children and friends who stop by to visit. Linnie can be found many afternoons in his favorite chair pouring over the Bible. He teaches a class at our church and spends hours in preparation for Sunday morning. I tease him sometimes about not having any tact. He doesn't have a lot of patience with people who don't take their Christian responsibilities seriously. We are both heart patients, but it doesn't slow us down much. We both ride our bikes during good weather and exercise daily.

Before I leave you I would like to share an example how, after forty-six years, our kids still pull together as a team. In recent years Linnie has been stumbling up or down our back steps leading to our yard. I shared this concern with Eddie one day.

"Eddie, would you mind building a rail going down both sets of steps to the back yard?" I asked him. "Daddy sometimes misses the next step down and falls."

"Sure, Mom, I'll get right on it."

The next thing I knew, Eddie showed us architectural plans for not just a railing, but an elaborate ramp leading to our two back doors. "Mom, all of the kids have come together and are going to build this ramp for you and Dad. We have all obligated our upcoming Saturdays for as long as it takes, to get this project done and have already taken up an offering to pay for it. The only thing you have to do is feed us when we are here," Eddie added.

I blinked and my eyes filled with tears. This was truly a labor of love. Linnie and I watched the children work many Saturdays on adapting door frames, fitting new moldings, and assembling boards for the frame. The women shoveled dirt and hammered like the men. A beautiful flower bed was also landscaped as part of the project. I hope, in years to come, to fill the bed with beautiful amaryllis blooms!" The new ramp provides us access to both doors with safety and ease. This truly exemplifies the kind of people our eight kids are.

In closing, I would be remiss if I didn't share Linnie's and my formula for success. When we married, it wasn't just the union of two people who were in love. It brought together three – God, Linnie, and me. God states this truth in Ecclesiastes 4:12b "*A cord of three strands is not easily torn apart.*" This has been the central theme throughout my story. It's my heart's cry! If you are a young couple reading this book, remember that it truly takes three. And the effort will bring you abundant love, abounding joy, and a peace that passes all understanding.

CPSIA information can be obtained
at www.ICGtesting.com
Printed in the USA
BVHW030948230719
553861BV00013B/3/P